350
<del>10</del>
c+7x

5-6-64

Sparks

(60-11576)

JULIA S. TUTWILER
AND SOCIAL PROGRESS

JULIA TUTWILER AS VASSAR STUDENT

Julia S. Tutwiler

AND SOCIAL PROGRESS
IN ALABAMA

ANNE GARY PANNELL
and DOROTHEA E. WYATT

1961 UNIVERSITY OF ALABAMA PRESS

*To the memory of those who have
believed in education as the road
to the American ideal*

'SPEND AND BE SPENT FOR OTHERS' SAKE!'
WHEN ONCE THIS JOY IS KNOWN
'TWERE HARD ITS SWEETNESS TO FORSAKE
AND LIVE FOR SELF ALONE.

Julia S. Tutwiler

Preface

IN THE BUSTLE of our present-day world we rarely take the time to inquire about the origin of the customs and the institutions that are our heritage. Such familiar social organizations as the public school and the state university we accept without wondering who were responsible for their establishment and development. If we think about these matters at all, we conjecture that some alert individuals recognized the problems, devised the solutions, and secured their adoption. Thus the evolution of social institutions, when viewed in retrospect, seems easy, straightforward, even obvious. Yet in actuality the process of social change is slow, halting, and difficult. Nor can the accomplishments always be attributed directly to the efforts of particular individuals. Indeed it is a characteristic of our American way of life that so much has been done by so many persons who remain unknown to recorded history.

This is particularly true when we consider the development of the American educational system. Many thousands of persons have contributed their ideas and their labors to the growth of American education. In most cases, however, there is no actual written record of the specific contributions of particular persons. The very extent of the stage and the multitude of the participants precludes that. Yet here and there we can distinguish the rare person, the pathfinder, the leader. And in reviewing the story of the accomplishments of this individual we gain useful information about a particular scene and a particular group of persons. In turn, this specific detail helps to fill in and define the larger background for a truer focus on state, regional, and national developments.

This book seeks to portray the life of one of the many men and women who have contributed to the betterment of Alabama and its people. In this case, the written word seeks only to record more surely for posterity the record already revered in Alabama of Julia Strudwick Tutwiler. The period of her life from 1841 to 1916 spans the eras of King Cotton, the War Between the States, Reconstruction, and the New South. Nurtured amid the best ante-bellum traditions of the Old South, she spent her adult life in educational and social reform activities. Inspired by an abiding faith in Christian teachings, stimulated by an exceptionally rich educational background, and possessed of a deep love for humanity, Julia Tutwiler was active in many fields. Spread over a long lifetime are such varied accomplishments as the following: the development of a campaign against alcoholism; the improvement of the state penal system to provide better care and rehabilitation for inmates; the words of the Alabama state song; the expansion of state-supported teacher training institutions; the introduction of vocational courses for women; the admission of women to the state university; the establishment of a state-supported college for women; and the encouragement of various organizations for charitable, educational, and social purposes.

In their search for material concerning Miss Tutwiler the authors unfortunately have not located any extensive collection of autobiographical materials, letters, or letters to her. Very possibly her own modesty coupled with the destruction by fire in 1896 of her parents' home at Greene Springs School helps to explain the paucity of source material. The authors are indebted to many individuals and many libraries for assistance in the accumulation of the sources that have been used in this book. In the appendix will be found a full description of these materials and specific acknowledgments.

Joint authors owe to their readers a word or two in explanation of their relative responsibilities and roles. The original design for this biography, the accumulation of the source materials, and the first version of the manuscript were the special contributions of Anne Gary Pannell. Dorothea E. Wyatt provided information on social and educational developments and assistance in the preparation of the final draft of the manuscript. Both authors, however, are jointly responsible for the text as it now stands.

This preface would not be complete without a special expression of gratitude for the listening ear and helpful comment of friends and colleagues in Tuscaloosa, Alabama, Lake Angelus, Michigan, and Sweet Briar, Virginia.

Anne Gary Pannell is under a special debt of gratitude to the Research Committee of the University of Alabama, which awarded her generous research grants 1945-1949 and has waited patiently for the completion of this manuscript. She wishes to express in particular her gratitude to the Committee's former Secretary, Mrs. W. K. E. James, for her unfailing kindnesses through these years.

Anne Gary Pannell
Sweet Briar, Virginia
Dorothea E. Wyatt
Flint, Michigan

September 1, 1957
March 1960

Contents

Illustrations

1. Daughter of the South

CHILDHOOD AND EARLY YEARS:
1841-1865

JULIA STRUDWICK TUTWILER, southern educator and humanitarian, was born in Alabama in 1841 during the heady period when the cultivation of cotton brought a sense of prosperity and security and encouraged a way of life that was rural, yet aristocratic and cultured. Those who have been privileged to be born in the South are particularly aware of the importance of family, tradition, and environment. And it is probably true that the cultural forces at work in the South during her youth were exceptionally strong and homogeneous. There was a charming simplicity about life in those years. The goals were few and clear. Young boys looked forward to being Christian cultured gentlemen who would draw their substance from the soil or in service to such time-honored institutions as the church, the army, and the professions. Girls were destined to be wives and mothers. Women were admired for their beauty, charm and manners, and for their grace and accomplishments in the home and on the plantation. In such a structured and stable society there was little to encourage an individual to depart from the accepted and traditional patterns.

The question naturally arises how Julia Tutwiler was drawn into an active life as an educator and a reformer. The strongest motivation came from within herself, from her own ethical and humanitarian convictions. It took idealism and courage to advocate social change in the South during the latter decades of the nineteenth century. Only a person of rare determination and principle could overcome the indifference, the discouragement, and the failure which fell to the lot of most reformers. Julia Tutwiler was well prepared for this by her family background. It was Julia's father, Henry Tutwiler, who had the greatest influence on her and provided the strongest single source of inspiration. By the force of his own character, his deep spiritual interests, and the breadth of his learning, he opened both her heart and her mind during her early formative years. By giving her the opportunity to pursue academic subjects of a nature and complexity then usually reserved to young men, he whetted her appetite for additional study. Further, the fact that his own educational training and experience had been varied encouraged her in later years to be unusually sympathetic to new educational ideas and theories. To the extent that Henry Tutwiler was an educational innovator and leader his daughter felt encouraged to seek out in later life new ideas and impressions and to advocate changes. There is no doubt that the influences associated with her home life and with her father helped to make this southern woman a nationally known educational administrator and advocate of social reform.

Henry Tutwiler had been born in Harrisonburg, Rockingham County, Virginia, in 1807. He was a descendant of pioneer stock that had earlier settled in Pennsylvania and probably had come originally from one of the German-speaking Swiss cantons. Much of his early education he had gained through his own efforts. When the University of Virginia opened its doors in 1825, he was one of the small company of young men who formed the first class. In later years, Tutwiler spoke with affectionate appreciation of the stimulus he had gained from his studies at this University and from the privilege afforded him occasionally of attending dinners given by Thomas Jefferson, then in his last years but devoted to the welfare of the institution he had done so much to found.[1]

In 1828, at the age of twenty, Tutwiler was gradu

ated from the University of Virginia. He then went
on to graduate study, thereafter receiving one of the
first Master of Arts degrees awarded by the University. While teaching in a small academy in the
neighborhood of Charlottesville, he was appointed
one of the first four faculty members of the newly
opened University of Alabama. A talented and en-
gaging young man of 23, Tutwiler found that the
duties of a professor were extensive and challenging.
They ranged from the responsibility of teaching
classes in various subjects to the obligation of su-
pervising in minute detail the activities of students
in and out of class. His keen interest in the welfare
of his students, the breadth of his training, and the
distinction of his intellectual attainments marked
young Tutwiler as a teacher and scholar of promise.
His students liked him and referred with approval
to his modest and affable manner and to the ease
with which they might approach him. In the summer of 1837 he resigned his professorship at the
University to accept an appointment at Marion, Alabama.[2] Subsequently, in 1840, he accepted a position as professor of mathematics and chemistry at
La Grange College, a Methodist institution in Lime-
stone County in northern Alabama.

While at the University, Tutwiler in 1835 had
married Julia Ashe. It was when he was on the
faculty of La Grange College that Julia, the most
famous of his eleven children, was born on August

15, 1841, in Tuscaloosa, where her mother had been visiting her family. Most of Julia's early life centered around Havana, a small community then in Greene County (now in Hale), about 25 miles south of the town of Tuscaloosa. It was here, when Julia was almost six years old, that her father established his Greene Springs School, one of the first and best preparatory schools in the state. Although Alabama was slow to develop a system of free public elementary and secondary schools, private initiative was responsible for the establishment of at least 250 academies in the period between 1820 and 1860. In his selection of a small village in Greene County in the fertile Black Belt, Tutwiler displayed an acumen equal to that of his prosperous planter neighbors. In this period Greene County was one of the richest and most prosperous cotton-producing areas in the entire South. In addition, in cultural matters the county ranked high, for in the years before 1865 it was second among the counties in the total number of young men attending the University of Alabama.

In establishing his private academy Tutwiler hoped to develop a school where subjects might be taught with a range in content and difficulty previously obtainable only in colleges. In the selection of subjects to teach, methods of instruction, and teachers he displayed a conscientious care for the educational growth of his pupils. Students were to be treated as individuals and not forced into any

rigid pattern. At the Greene Springs School, the
scholars were encouraged to proceed at their own
rate and to enter the classes for which they were
prepared. Corporal punishment was forbidden.
When moral persuasion had no good results, Tutwiler scorned the use of force and simply required
the incorrigible student to go home. His students
spoke of his "sweet, benign, tender, sun-shiny presence" and remembered how he endeavored to develop their interest in current literature and scientific
and political thought as well as in the more prosaic
subjects of study. He hoped to put the primary
emphasis on the usefulness of information and not
just its acquisition. The importance of having qualified teachers to instruct the young was also empha-
sized by Tutwiler. At a time when foreign languages
were taught in a bookish manner, he encouraged
the use of natural and lifelike methods of instruction. His own study and experience as a teacher of
mathematics and science had convinced him of the
need to provide apparatus for observation and experiment in subjects like botany, chemistry, and
astronomy. The Greene Springs Academy had what
was for the period a fine telescope of considerable
magnification. It was with the use of this telescope
that Tutwiler had the pleasure and distinction on
May 12, 1866, of discovering a small "temporary"
star in the constellation of the Northern Crown,
now known as T Corona Borealis. New ideas and

vigorous methods in conjunction with his personal qualities and attainments soon won a wide reputation for Tutwiler and his school.[3]

The site that Tutwiler chose for his school had previously been a popular health resort. The existing buildings were refitted to serve as the school. During the years to come improvements were made and additional acreage purchased until Tutwiler owned about 1,500 acres of land. Only scanty details now exist. It is known that a chapel and a library building stood to the right of the Tutwiler home. The family residence was a rambling one-story house with a basement. By 1854 there were two rows of student dormitories containing in all a total of 25 rooms.

It was in this setting that Julia and her sisters and brothers had their upbringing. Family memories agree that the home was warm, friendly, hospitable, and cultured.[4] There were many visitors to enliven the days and to provide recreation and stimulation for the young people. The atmosphere was conducive to learning. Julia herself was slow to start to read but once she had mastered the skill she became a constant reader. Even at this early age she was influenced by the example set by her father. She early exhibited an interest in teaching and sought to show her younger sister, then only three and a half, how to read. Naturally such a premature effort failed to meet with success. But it did show the direction in which the twig was bent. Somewhat later, Julia organized small classes for the slave children at Greene Springs and continued with her instruction until they could read.

Very early in her life Julia Tutwiler manifested what was to be a continuing and absorbing interest in literature, particularly in its imaginative and romantic aspects. When she was seven her enthusiasm for William Collins' "The Passions: An Ode for Music" led her to direct her sister Katherine in a re-enactment of the poem. While Julia (or "Jule" as she was then called) recited the lines

> Next Anger rush'd; his Eyes on fire,
> In Lightnings own'd his secret Stings:
> In one rude Clash he struck the Lyre,
> And swept with hurried Hand the Strings.

Katherine was told to personify "Anger" and to run about the family garden and snatch a water dipper near their mother's flower bed. This spirited action led Mrs. Tutwiler, who was attempting to garden, to insist that the two girls go elsewhere to play.

At another time, Jule was deeply moved when quoting from another of her literary favorites, Schiller's play about Joan of Arc, *The Maid of Orleans*. In an intense outburst of feeling she declared that, like Joan, she intended never to marry but instead planned to devote herself to a life dedicated to the service of others. There were occasions in her childhood when Julia's love for literature was displayed in her own efforts to be a writer. When she was nine years old she joined with her two older sisters in producing a little magazine called "The Monthly Rose." This was designed as a replica of the adult literary magazines the Tutwiler children were familiar with in their father's library. The children's magazine, written on long, blue-tinted paper, contained stories, poems, funny sayings, and editorials. Many years later Julia expressed dismay at the immaturity and lack of depth in these early compositions. She spoke of these first literary efforts as "a sort of parrot mixture" of all that she had read.

Thus it was that Julia Tutwiler's childhood was spent in a happy family circle. When the time came to plan for her formal education, she was fortunate to have the sympathetic encouragement of a father who was a teacher himself and who was progressive enough to believe that girls, too, should be educated. Along with her sisters and a number of daughters of neighboring families Julia attended classes in the Greene Springs School. The girls had the same assignments as the boys and attended classes and recited with them. Their study halls, however, were separate. Tutwiler was indeed a pioneer in thus providing liberally for the education of girls in the same classes with boys. Such a procedure was rare in the United States in the 1840's and 1850's, par-

ticularly so in the conservative Deep South. The
academic association with boys gave Julia an acquaintance with many male contemporaries who
were later to be friends or foes in her various endeavors. This school experience also gave her direct
evidence that girls as well as boys could benefit from
equal educational opportunities. It was an important influence later on in encouraging her to work
for co-education.

The religious convictions of her father also had a
deep and enduring effect on Julia. He was a man
who believed fully in the validity of the Christian
concept of the equal worth of every soul. He took
seriously the basic precepts of Christianity and
sought to combine religious teachings with character
development. Owing to the fact that his school was
in the country at some distance from churches, he
assumed a large share of responsibility for the religious instruction of his students and family. On
Sundays, for example, he conducted religious services. At one session it was his custom to deliver a
short moral lecture or to read an extract from an
interesting sermon. At the gathering after supper
he usually expected each student to be able to quote
some line, stanza, or short poem containing a moral
or religious idea or a selection from the Bible. In
such a pious atmosphere a warm and impressionable
girl like Julia could not help being imbued with
religious ideas and with a reverence for the Bible.

As she approached her late teens in the last years of the 1850's Julia seemed a fortunate young lady. Her social position as the daughter of the proprietor of an esteemed academy in the wealthy Black Belt was assured. The degree of prosperity of the Tutwiler family can only be surmised. It is known that Henry Tutwiler owned "more than 20 slaves" at the outbreak of the War. Figures are entirely lacking as to family or school finances. However, the head of another Alabama academy estimated in 1858 that with an investment of about $8,000 in school property he was able to clear between $3,000 and $5,000 yearly. This was at a time when the average teacher's salary in Macon County, Alabama, was less than $400 per year. There is evidence that Tutwiler's school was unusually successful both in educational and financial aspects. He was reported to be a man of excellent judgment in practical affairs and to have accumulated a considerable fortune as a result of his educational enterprise and his wise investments. Thus he was in a position to finance a further step in the education and development of his talented daughter. This was to provide her with schooling away from home.[5]

Prevailing sentiment in the South during the 1850's was strongly critical of secular education, co-education, and the kinds of education found in northern schools. Few respectable southerners wished to risk sending a young woman to a northern

place of learning where she might become infected
with radical vagaries such as feminism, liberalism,
or humanitarianism. The sweep of romanticism
and the growth of the cult of chivalry in the South
in the decades from 1830 to 1860 had reinforced
the traditional idea that woman's place was in the
home, that she should be highly feminine and look
up to the male as her protector. As if these beliefs
were not sufficiently restraining, the rising tide of
southern nationalism strongly militated against the
idea that the South might be lacking in any desirable
form of intellectual or cultural experience.

But Henry Tutwiler and his daughter had minds
of their own and they departed from the pattern of
their planter neighbors by deciding on a northern
educational venture. It thus came about that for
two winters just prior to the outbreak of the War
Julia attended a boarding school in Philadelphia
conducted by a Madame Maroteau.[6] It was here,
where the use of French was a daily experience in
the classroom and at table, that Julia's strong interest
in the study and teaching of modern foreign languages was awakened.

The outbreak of the War in April of 1861 made
it necessary for Julia to return home. Tutwiler was
a Whig in politics and opposed to secession but took
no active part in the political struggles. The Tutwiler family's slaves were treated with consideration
and never sold. Indeed, both Julia and her father

had endeavored, contrary to Alabama law, to give some facility in reading and writing to those who were interested in bettering themselves.[7] But when Alabama seceded, both father and daughter responded loyally and supported the Confederacy. At twenty, Julia was filled with patriotic emotion and enthusiasm and besought her father for permission to leave home to be a nurse for wounded Confederate soldiers. Making use of a skill that was to be hers through life, she composed in 1862 a short poem[8] in an effort to win her father's assent:

LET ME GO: THE WAR DRUM SOUNDETH

Let me go: the war drum soundeth,
And the bugle screams afar.
Hark! now louder, clearer soundeth
Deadlier music from the war.

See my countrymen lie bleeding;
On the gory sands they lie,
Messengers of Death still speeding,
O'er their heads a burning sky.

Shall I be a baseborn coward,
Harder hearted than the foe?
See, my country, Duty calls me:
Dearest Father, let me go!

But the father was adamant in his refusal and none of the Tutwiler daughters was permitted to serve as a Confederate nurse. Instead the family made a closely knit circle and each did what he or she could to keep the school and the home in operation. Julia

now entered for the first time upon her formal career as a teacher and taught the students still in residence. She also found time to give instruction to less favored white children in the neighborhood who could not afford to be regular students. Accompanied by a small brother she often rode on horseback as far as five miles into the countryside to help ambitious children learn to read and write.

The struggles and privations of the long war years at times caused Julia's warm spirit to be chilled under the continuing worries and burdens. At one Christmas season, when the Negroes were gone and the sisters were washing dishes, Julia remarked that if she thought she'd have to do this kind of thing the rest of her life, she'd rather die. But her spirits soon revived and she busied herself with writing and producing several plays. The casts of these plays were made up of students at the school and neighbors. Admission was charged and the proceeds went to help local families whose husbands and relatives were at the front.

On other occasions Julia read aloud when the women of the family were gathered in the evening around the table to prepare bandages for use in army hospitals. She read dramatically, using her voice and hands to thrill her listeners. As in her childhood, Schiller remained a particular favorite, especially *The Maid of Orleans*.

During the war years Julia also performed in fitting fashion the role of plantation mistress by caring for old and incapacitated Negro family servants. Her former nurse, who had been freed by her father some years previously because the Alabama climate had been too severe for her asthma, now returned to the Tutwiler home as a last refuge before death. Julia faithfully cared for this old Negro, Aunt Amy. So, too, did she watch over another old servant who had no other person to take an interest in her welfare. Here is foreshadowed the keen interest that Julia Tutwiler was later to take in the welfare of the destitute.

With the end of the War in April of 1865 Julia, like others in her native state, was faced with the necessity of making plans for the future. Now approaching her twenty-fourth year, she wished above all to renew her educational training and she wished once again to study outside the South. It is likely that at this time she had not yet decided upon a career as distinct from marriage. She was not particularly inclined to the usual social activities of a woman of her age and upbringing. There is even some suggestion that she was not very attractive in appearance and that her sisters outshone her in social charm. It probably was an inner urge not yet clearly defined that drove her on to seek new educational and cultural experiences. She could not help being aware of the hardships and privations that faced young white girls in the Black Belt of Alabama now

that the economic props of the old plantation economy had been removed. Formerly the planter
fathers had been able to afford some educational
opportunities, but now the prospect was bleak. After
the War, only a few families had resources to finance
extended education. As a privileged person, Julia
was conscious of the need to gain something practical and useful both to her and to her beloved
Alabama.

2. Restless Searcher

STUDY AND TRAVEL IN AMERICA
AND ABROAD: 1865-1876

THE YEARS FROM 1865 to 1876 mark the period in Julia Tutwiler's life during which she slowly developed her interests and ambitions. Although she loved Alabama and respected its traditions, she was aware of a paucity of opportunities. Indeed she was not alone in thinking that the people of the South needed new educational experiences. There were many voices raised to suggest that adequate instruction in science, technology, business, and other vocations was lacking. Moreover, the general uncertainty and restlessness after 1865 encouraged Julia to begin a course of travel and study in the United States and Europe.

It was fortunate that Henry Tutwiler was able

to finance the cost of his daughter's travel and study. The Greene Springs School had remained open during the war years and had suffered no serious physical damage. Unlike most of his contemporaries he was able, therefore, to secure with relative ease an immediate source of income. Furthermore there were some funds he had earlier invested in Philadelphia that were available for use.

In the summer of 1865 Julia and her older sister Margaret journeyed to Philadelphia. Here Julia continued her studies at Madame Maroteau's French and English School. The sisters enjoyed such cultural pleasures as the opera and the company of congenial friends but they found the general atmosphere to be empty and lonely. Julia sought to assuage her sense of isolation by writing poems, a practice she followed throughout her life. In these poems she expressed a warm devotion to the South and to her family and friends. Underneath these expressions of attachment to the old and familiar there is detected a note of personal uncertainty, of sadness, yet of devotion to duty. One of these poems, written in August of 1865 and entitled "The Vanquished Patriot's Prayer" contains the following stanzas:

> Ruler of nations! bow thine ear!
> I cannot understand
> Thy ways; but Thou wilt heed this prayer
> For my beloved land.

> Teach me to sorrow with my land
>> Yet not to hate her foe,
> To bow submissive to Thy hand,
>> Which dealt the chastening blow.
>
> Pilgrims and strangers in the world,
>> No land to call our own:
> Our banner from its station hurled,
>> Our Freedom from her throne.
>
> Let us not try in scenes of mirth
>> For surcease to our grief;
> Help us to turn to Heaven from earth,
>> Seek only there relief.

Another poem from these gloomy Philadelphia days, untitled, was designed as a hymn and contains these revealing stanzas:

> 'Spend and be spent for others' sake!'
> When once this joy is known
> 'Twere hard its sweetness to forsake
> And live for self alone.
>
> Not mine, alas! to have attained
> Such loftiness of soul,
> But thither fair my hopes would tend
> As to their distant goal.

Whatever it was that Julia was seeking at this period in her life, neither Philadelphia nor Madame Maroteau's school was able to furnish. It is not known just what reasons led her in the winter of 1865-66 to decide to enter Vassar College. This was then a newly opened institution attracting much attention among those who advocated higher education for women. It is possible there was some connection between the Tutwiler family and Milo P. Jewett, who had been closely associated with Matthew Vassar in the founding of the college. Years before, Jewett had established a female academy in Marion, Alabama. Conceivably Henry Tutwiler had known him in the late 1830's when both were living in the same town. In any event, Julia obtained the necessary funds from the sale of some of her father's investments in Philadelphia. Late in January of 1866 she arrived at Poughkeepsie, New York, to take up her studies at the new college.

The available records do not indicate just what academic status Julia had at Vassar College. In the beginning years students were not classified until they had been in residence for some time. One of the requirements for advanced status was a prescribed mastery in traditional subjects such as Latin and Greek equal to that expected in the men's colleges. It is possible, though by no means certain, that her studies under her father and her teaching experience did entitle Julia to academic rank as an "advanced standing" student. However, of the more than 300 young women who entered Vassar in the first academic year probably no more than 20 or 30 were qualified to rank as juniors and most of these had previously been teachers.[1]

One of Julia's happiest memories of the half year spent at Vassar College was the part she took in the first Founder's Day celebration, arranged on April 29, 1866, in honor of the birthday of Matthew Vassar. It was an occasion well suited to bring forth her creative and poetic efforts. The benign patron of women's education, then in his seventy-fourth year, was the subject of tribute by this warm-hearted and idealistic student. She played a prominent part in the arrangements for the celebration and composed the verses for the song in his honor. Entitled "Our Father and Our Friend," it was sung at the festivities and contained the lines:

> In Heaven Angels sing God's praise—on Earth Women and all good Men sing yours.
> Long may you live to hear it, is the prayer of a Stranger.

Instead of returning to Vassar in the autumn of 1866 to continue her studies, Julia accepted a position as a member of the faculty at the Greensboro Female Academy in Greensboro, county seat of Hale County, Alabama.[2] The reasons for this decision are not known. It may be that she believed she was inadequately prepared to undertake the course of study at Vassar. On the other hand, she may have considered herself too old and too mature to continue in the atmosphere of a women's boarding college. There is the possibility that the Tutwiler family felt the pinch of the difficult years of Reconstruction when taxes were heavy and specie was scarce. Very likely the appointment as "Assistant in the Academic Department" represented an opportunity to gain a livelihood and to further her teaching career in a place not too far from home.

As was true of most educational institutions in Alabama at this time, the Greensboro Academy was struggling to make ends meet. The school buildings were in need of repair, and books and equipment were sadly deficient. When the principal resigned in the summer of 1867, the trustees elected Julia as his successor. This was a liberal step in the Deep South of this period and is evidence of her ability and personality. The local paper approved of the appointment and voiced satisfaction with her qualifications.[3]

During the two years from 1867 to 1869 that Julia Tutwiler held her first school administrative post she proceeded to make a number of changes in accord with her views. Her interest in the teaching of foreign language is indicated by the fact that she canceled the extra fee which had been previously charged for the study of Latin, French, and German. She displayed a concern for the fundamentals. Students were not permitted to elect Latin until they had demonstrated a competence in the structure, history, and practical use of English. She also endeavored to collect a special fee in order to build up the library and to obtain maps. There was no grading and in the academic department Julia taught all of the more advanced pupils.

Perhaps the greatest success during the brief period she was at the Greensboro Academy came in the encouragement she gave to student festivals and in her participation in community activities. One notable occasion was the school May Day celebration in 1869 when the students presented an elaborate cantata "with an underlying moral." She wrote the allegorical prologue and the songs. With other citizens in the town she was active in the project to erect a Soldiers' Monument for the Confederate dead in the local cemetery.

It is unknown just what was the decisive factor in the summer of 1869 that led her to resign this principalship at the Greensboro Academy and to become once again a teaching assistant at the Greene Springs School. Possibly she was discouraged by the continuing financial problem and by the heavy teaching and administrative burdens. Very likely the determining factors were her desire to be at home with her father and to work as a teacher in his school amid pleasant personal surroundings. Whatever the reason for the decision to leave the Greensboro Academy and return to Greene Springs, her sojourn at home was relatively brief. Little is known about her work during these years from 1869 to 1872 other than the fact that she assisted in the lower grades at first and then in the higher. Apparently she also taught some special classes in ancient and modern languages.

Julia's next educational experience brought her to her father's native state of Virginia for a year of private study. It would appear that she felt a strong need to improve her proficiency in foreign language. Perhaps she had in mind preparing herself either to return to Vassar College or to undertake travel or study abroad. One of her brothers was then in his last year of study at Washington and Lee University and she accompanied him back to Lexington. There she lived with a relative and took private instruction in foreign languages from the professors. Later on she praised the tutoring she received at this time. She credited her year's stay in Lexington with helping her to learn the latest and most improved methods of language instruction and pronunciation.

It was during this stay in Virginia that she was inspired to write "When the Laurels Bloom," one of her best known and most admired poems. This she composed to honor Commodore Matthew Fontaine Maury, the noted oceanographer who died early in 1873. For a brief period of time in the summer of 1871 Maury had served as President of the University of Alabama. At the time of his death he was a professor at Virginia Military Institute in Lexington. Eager to pay tribute to this distinguished southerner and to record his love for the mountain laurel, Julia Tutwiler wrote the following poem:

WHEN THE LAURELS BLOOM

Round his dying couch his dearest
Weeping, praying, ministering stood—
All the fondest and the nearest,
Of his race and kindred blood.
Sailors on the distant billow—
Men of every race and land
Blessed the head upon that pillow—
Blessed that tireless patient hand.

.   .   .   .

He had seen the Aurora streaming
O'er the trackless waste of white—
Watched the iceberg's fearful gleaming
Through the wondrous Polar night.
Tropic lands had poured before him
Wasteful wealth of life and love;
Laden palm-trees bending o'er him;
At his feet the coral grove.

Through the night-watch on the ocean,
As upon the deck he turned
Weary of the wave's wild motion—
Not for these his heart had yearned.
But the Blue Ridge Mountain passes
Rose before him—either side
Clustering thick with rosy masses—
Laurel blooms—the mountain's pride.

Now when life's long voyage was over,
And the blessed port in sight
Still his heart looked back—a lover
To each blue and lessening height.
"If you lay me with my kindred,
Take me not in winter's gloom;

Bear me, dear ones, through my mountains,
Yonder, when the laurels bloom."

"When the laurels bloom," O, sailor!
Sayest thou "When the laurels bloom"?
They *are* blooming now and ever,
Fadeless on thine honored tomb.[4]

In the summer of 1873 as she neared her thirty-second birthday, Julia went on a tour of Europe that lengthened into a visit of several years.[5] Together with a brother, she was a member of a fairly large conducted party of several hundred ministers and public school teachers mostly from northern and western states. During their travels in England Julia had an interesting experience of the kind that well illustrates both the warmth of her personality and the inquiring nature of her mind. She had been disappointed to learn that the few tickets available to admit women to observe Parliament, then in session, had long since been distributed. Late in the evening of her last day in London, she was unexpectedly called upon by a relative of Commodore Maury who wished to express for his family their appreciation for the poem "When the Laurels Bloom." When Julia told General Maury of her unfulfilled wish to attend Parliament, he responded by saying he would attempt to secure admission for her that very evening. Maury and Julia hastened to Parliament where he found an acquaintance, a Conservative member from Birkenhead named John

Laird. He was one of the partners in the famous English shipbuilding firm that had built several commerce raiders for the Confederacy. Among the most famous of these so-called "Laird rams" was the *Alabama*. In her account Julia identified this gentleman as "Mr. Layard," a phonetic rendering of his name. Upon being introduced to her, Laird politely asked, "From what state are you, Miss Tutwiler?" The question immediately had overtones. The United States and Britain had just settled a long dispute over the question of responsibility for the damages to American shipping caused by the *Alabama* and her sister ships. In 1872 Britain had agreed to pay the sum of $15,500,000 to the United States in settlement of these "Alabama claims." Julia was at once aware of the humor of the situation. Demurely she replied, "Indeed, Mr. Layard, I don't like to tell you!"

Whereupon Laird is reported to have laughed heartily and replied, "Ah! You need not tell me now, I know without being told. But in spite of 'Alabama Claims' you see I am back again in Parliament."

Fortunately Laird was able to secure admission for Julia Tutwiler to the ladies' balcony of the House of Commons. She sat there, next to Laird's daughter, and saw but did not hear the great leaders, Gladstone and Disraeli. It seemed to Julia that the members of the House of Commons were too halt-

ing and jerky in their style of oratory and method
of presenting material. She came away pleased and
stimulated by her experience but convinced that
American orators were far ahead of their English
counterparts.

Julia's tour went on to Vienna and on the way
back the party made the usual tour of the Rhine.
By this time, the restrictive and confining aspects
of the tour and of membership in a "party of tour-
ists" had begun to pall on the lively and inquisitive
Julia. She longed to be free of the stodgy admoni-
tions of the guide and of the trite comments of her
companions. For some weeks, she had been search-
ing for a suitable place where she might perfect her
knowledge of foreign languages and of methods of
teaching. Her brief tour of Europe had served to
convince her that Germany was a leader in educational matters and she had come in the course of her
travels to admire the German people above all other
Europeans. Of course, part of this appreciation
may have come from the fact that Julia was proud
of her German cultural heritage.

Undoubtedly Julia's interest in Germany was
prompted in part by the nineteenth century American esteem for German educational achievements.
In the years from 1815 to 1870 Prussia had developed a system of public elementary schools per-
meated by a strong nationalistic tone. It was in this
period that Pestalozzian ideas as to the development

of the mental faculties, training through the senses, and the power of education to transform society continued to have wide acceptance in theory. In actual practice the Prussian state had been most interested in the adoption of subject matter and of methods of instruction that would be useful to the growth of Prussia. Subjects like geography, history, German speech, and music were taught as much for patriotic as for educational reasons. The practical values of drawing and arithmetic had been given emphasis. Great stress was placed upon religion in the public schools with a shift from the eighteenth century emphasis on church doctrine and the catechism to such values as moral earnestness, humility, self-sacrifice, and obedience to authority.

After the establishment of the new German Empire in 1870 under Prussian leadership, it was understandable that German educational policies would continue to be nationalistic, paternal, practical, and authoritarian. The purpose of educational legislation under the German Empire was not to make the German people critical thinkers and independent personalities but to make them orderly, obedient, vocationally efficient, and personally satisfied with their status in life. In this process of developing and improving their system of education in the latter part of the nineteenth century, German educational leaders continued to win the respect of observers from other countries who could not help but admire some of their aims and many of their results.

Julia Tutwiler was not the only American woman of note in this period who sought to further her education in Germany. M. Carey Thomas, later to attain distinction as Dean and President of Bryn Mawr College, began her studies in Germany in the autumn of 1879. Her motivation and ambition, however, set her apart from Julia. From the first, Carey Thomas had been intolerant of any form of higher education that did not match that open to men. Hence she did not rest content until in November, 1882, she received from the University of Zürich the same Ph. D. degree that was awarded to men. It was her goal "to remedy the great failing of American women teachers, and most men—their want of scholarship—and to advance the cause of women by her own achievement. . . ."[6]

No such strong feminist ambition dominated Julia Tutwiler. Her whole background militated against unladylike competitive activity in professional fields hitherto reserved for men. At the time she sought to study in Germany, no German woman was welcome at or officially permitted to attend a German institution of higher learning. Quite possibly, too, Julia realized that her previous academic training, particularly in the classics and modern languages, was too weak to justify her seeking the special favor of attendance at lectures in the German universities, a privilege sometimes granted to foreign women. When Carey Thomas' father was pondering whether to let her study abroad, he wrote for advice in 1879 to President Andrew D. White of Cornell University, then serving as United States Minister to Germany. White replied that he did not approve of any young lady regularly attending lectures at a German university. He thought it best for Carey Thomas to live with a German family, perfect her knowledge of the German language, attend "certain lectures suitable to ladies," and travel.

Small wonder, therefore, that a sensitive southern gentlewoman should turn to a quiet and secluded place of practical training frequented by women. It may be that Julia's half year at Vassar College had sharply turned her interest away from the traditional type of institution of higher learning. Her life in the South during the hard years of Reconstruction had the effect of suggesting to her the values in vocational training. When one of Julia's travel companions told her of the teacher training work of the Diakonessen Anstalt, run by an order of Protestant sisters of charity, she promptly made her decision. She would put herself under the direction of these sisters and endeavor to gain the same inspiration and training that Florence Nightingale had experienced during her stay in 1851.[7]

The decision made, Julia Tutwiler lost no time hastening to the Institute of Deaconesses. It was

located in the small town of Kaiserswerth, on the
right bank of the Rhine, about six miles south of
Düsseldorf. When she reached Düsseldorf, she was
advised to wait for the next regular trip of the stage
coach or the steamer. She could brook no such de-
lay and despite her poor German and her inexpe-
rience in traveling alone she arranged to rent a hack
to take her on immediately to Kaiserswerth. Thus
it was that on the evening of August 7, 1873, Julia
Tutwiler requested admission to the Institute. The
sisters were naturally surprised. She was their first
American applicant and she had come without any
letters of introduction or recommendation. They
directed her to the village inn to stay until they
could decide upon her request for admission.

In this interval, Julia had time to become thoroughly familiar with the village. The Institute consisted of several units, including a deaconess house,
a hospital, an infant school, a training school for
teachers, an orphanage for girls, an asylum for the
aged, the infirm, and the blind, and a retreat for
retired deaconesses. The impetus for the establishment of this training school and benevolent institution had come from a Lutheran pastor, Theodor
Fliedner, and his first wife, Friedericke Münster
Fliedner. Strongly moved by a desire to meet the
needs of the unfortunate, the Fliedners in the 1830's
had established the first unit, a small hospital, at
Kaiserswerth. They had undertaken also the recruit-

ment, training, and support of nurses. These women were dedicated to the service of the Lord and of the unfortunate, hence the religious title of deaconess. This Protestant order spread rather widely during the nineteenth century and attracted considerable interest in and out of Germany.

While Julia waited for the decision as to whether she might enter the training school, she proceeded with characteristic shrewd good humor to accustom herself, while still at the village inn, to the frugal meals she knew to be served at the Institute. She wrote home and recounted her experiences in tapering off from a ten course table d'hote meal by ordering "cafe," which consisted of a pot of coffee, a pitcher of hot milk, butter, and a plate of white and black bread. She took walks about the village and liked all that she saw of it and of the Germans. She was thrilled by the ruins of castle walls and towers along the Rhine and stirred by the folk tales concerning Frederick Barbarossa, whose early life had centered in the locality and who had been crowned German king at nearby Aix-la-Chapelle in 1152.

The deaconesses, impressed by the simplicity and the selflessness of their applicant, accepted Julia as a student in their training school for teachers. On August 14, 1873, she entered the normal school and found herself closely associated with women who out of a deep sense of Christian love had dedicated themselves to the alleviation of human suffering and to the advancement of mankind. The curriculum of the training school placed a major emphasis on methods of religious and moral instruction. Each student teacher had ample opportunity to put these theories into practice under supervision in the Institute schools for little children and for girls. All of this was practical and sincere and it struck a responsive chord in Julia's heart. Here, as in her father's school at Greene Springs, she found an emphasis placed upon the individuality of each person, whether deaconess, child, patient, or reformatory inmate. It was a simple life, well-organized, based upon a faith in Christian ideas and in active service.

Later, in describing her life at the Institute of Deaconesses, she characterized it as " 'plain living and high thinking' well carried out." Flowers, books, and music were the only luxuries, she thought, and even music had its practical side since it was regarded not only as a means to recreation but also as a tool in achieving educational objectives. As part of the normal school course in "house-wifery" Julia took her turn with the other trainees in serving meals and in preparing such items as coffee and soup. She also shared in the daily half hour of housekeeping and cleaning duties. Her favorite recreation was to walk through the gardens and the farm. The acres of beautifully cultivated grounds contained a rich variety of flowers and vegetables.

She admired the neat hedges that divided the various parts of the garden. The good view afforded of the Rhine with its traffic of boats and steamers never failed to please her.

In such a pastoral setting there was ample opportunity for Julia to carry out another of her simple pleasures, the observation and study of birds. She later reported:

Often, as I sat reading in a bower of the quaint garden on the banks of the Rhine, where flowers and vegetables mingling together made an object lesson on the mutual helpfulness of utility and beauty, I watched the little brown-clad singer [a nightingale] warbling his heart away not two yards above me. . . . If I sat very still the little singer's curiosity was aroused, and he hopped lightly down from twig to twig until he was on the ground. . . . If I could remain quite motionless he would come to my very feet, but if a breeze from the Rhine rustled the leaves of my book he would quickly lift his wings and seek a safe distance. Often at night when his song began I rose and knelt for hours at the window to listen to his music.[8]

Undoubtedly, the year spent at the Institute of Deaconesses in Kaiserswerth from the autumn of 1873 to the summer of 1874 was one of the most influential in molding the professional life of Julia Tutwiler. She participated directly in the work of a well-run educational and philanthropic institution. This experience heightened her humanitarian zeal and strengthened her faith in the processes of education. She witnessed the successful operation of a moral and vocational training program for the

women inmates of the prison. She also observed and
shared in the program of the school for the training
of teachers. She found an emphasis on the need of
organized play for children as well as the provision
of character training in all aspects of education. She
found, too, attention given to providing vocational
or industrial education so that women might find
honest and gainful employment.

In an address delivered on July 16, 1891, to the
annual meeting of the National Educational Association held in Toronto, Canada, Julia Tutwiler
described in detail her year in a German model
school. She conceded that the curriculum of the
Kaiserswerth normal school might seem limited because of its failure to include such subjects as Greek
or Latin, or any mathematics above arithmetic, or
anything more advanced in the natural sciences than
might be taught in an American kindergarten. She
firmly believed, however, that any such deficiencies
were more than made up by the excellence of instruction in other subjects. She described the normal school course of instruction as including

1. oral and written lessons in the German language
2. a thorough study of the masterpieces of German literature
3. hymnology
4. the history and geography of Europe, with major emphasis on Germany

5. the study of foreign languages, usually French, but often French and English
6. lectures on the methods of instruction and on child-training, with practice teaching under supervision
7. plain sewing and fancy-work
8. housewifery[9]

She had unstinted praise for some of the methods employed. For example, in most of the courses there were no textbooks available for student use. Hence there could be no "parrot teaching," or excessive dependence on rote memorization of textbook material. Julia drew a distinction between "logical memory" and "verbal memory" that may not be clear to later students of educational methods. She disapproved of "logical memory" because of its dependence on the memorization of a textbook. She approved of "verbal memory" which she identified with the careful study by a student of the notes taken down from the teacher's lecture. She commented favorably upon the strong emphasis given to the study of German literature and history.

In this summary of her year at this German normal school, Julia reluctantly admitted that the list of accomplishments might compare unfavorably with those in an American normal school. However, she went on to say

. . . yet I had to admire very much the type of women which [the Institute of Deaconesses] developed—gentle, thoughtful, intelligent women — clear-headed and open-minded, with the power to think accurately and to express their thoughts plainly. There was nothing muddled in their brains—nothing that indicated a mind surcharged with more than it could digest, and subsequently congested. I have seen something like this in the United States.

In this judgment, expressed almost seventeen years after her Kaiserswerth experience, Julia declared that the good results attained by the deaconesses in their teacher training Institute came not just from the simplicity and thoroughness of the curriculum. She believed that "at the risk of being old-fashioned and unprogressive, far behind the spirit of the age, I will say that I attribute the best results of this school to its Christian teaching."[10]

Upon the completion of her year of study in the teacher training school of the Institute of Deaconesses at Kaiserswerth, Julia remained in Europe for the next two years, 1874-76. Details are somewhat fragmentary and none too clear as to her life during this period. It would appear that she spent most of the time in or near Berlin, living with private families and attempting to continue her studies with a minimum of financial expense. It is probable that she also visited German university towns, such as Bonn and Göttingen, in order to attend lectures on German literature. Either in these years, or earlier during her stay at Kaiserswerth, she took and passed the examinations given by the Prussian government for the normal school teacher's certificate. At this time, the Prussian government required two examinations for teachers. The first, for provisional teachers, was given in the teachers' seminaries at the close of the school year and included all the subjects of the normal school course. After two years of experience, a male provisional teacher was eligible to take the second examination in order to secure tenure and promotion. Among the requirements of the second examination were a thesis on a pedagogical topic, evidence of successful classroom teaching, and an oral examination on the theories and practices of education. The examinations for women teachers were different and were specially designed because the teaching posts filled by women were of low rank and importance.

During these years of study in Germany, Julia was compelled to practice every economy in order to make her allowance from home go as far as possible. She quickly learned to make every cent count, particularly so in the purchase and care of her clothing. Apparently, during the year at Kaiserswerth Julia had only two good dresses, a "brown merino" and a "dark purple." When these faded from the strong sun and constant wear, she wrote home of her plans to have them dyed and made over to conform to the "neatness" so much insisted upon in that hard-working community. Julia came to admire the simplicity of "shirtwaists of striped calico with cuffs and collars of the same which

could be taken off" and skirts and overskirts of
"good waterproof." These years of enforced thrift
no doubt strengthened her conviction that American women wasted a great deal of money on dress.
She believed that almost any American girl who
would be very self-denying in her dress for two
years could save enough to spend a few months
abroad.

As a means of adding to her income and as a way
of giving expression to her new experiences and
ideas, Julia wrote a number of pieces for American
newspapers and magazines. In the June 1875 and
May 1876 issues of *St. Nicholas,* a well-known magazine for children, are to be found two of her stories.
She told of the kindergarten at Kaiserswerth and
of some of the games and songs of the German children in a story called "The Postman's Boy (A German Game for the Little Folks)." Another of her
German stories was "Christinchen's Answer," a simple tale of a schoolmaster who prepared the children
of his village for a visit by the king.

To Julia's German years belong at least two other
articles. These were entitled "Amber on the Shores
of the Baltic" and "On the Baltic in the Sea and on
the Shore," and they appeared in the June and
October 1876 issues of *Appleton's Journal.* The
material reveals a keen interest in German folklore
and in the German language and literature extend-
ing even to a brief period of experimentation in

spelling her name as "Tutweiler." It appears from
the content of these articles that Julia had spent a
happy seaside holiday with the family of a Lutheran
pastor at a place in or near the old town of Kolberg
in Pomerania. Here she enjoyed the usual seaside
and holiday activities of swimming, shopping for
souvenirs, and sightseeing. She went as far east as
Danzig and Königsberg and considered making a
visit to the Gulf of Bothnia in order to see its re-
puted wild beauty. In the course of her rambles
along the Baltic, she developed considerable interest
in amber and in the methods used by the fisher folk
in obtaining this valuable product of the sea.

Of far more merit and lasting renown was her
authorship sometime in the fall of 1873 of the poem
"Alabama." It was at this time that Julia was particularly lonesome for the relatives at home and for
the sights of her native state. Her study of German
literature and history and her own love of poetry
led her to try to capture in words the devotion she
felt. The immediate inspiration came to her as she
sat in her room studying and overheard a group of
German children pass by singing "Deutschland über
Alles."[11]

The first, and unauthorized, version of Julia Tutwiler's poem "Alabama" appeared in the *Tuscaloosa
Times* on January 27, 1875. It was accompanied by
a note to the effect that it was to be sung to the air
of "Deutschland über Alles." By the time Julia

returned home from Germany in 1876 she found
her poem widely reprinted. This encouraged her
to perfect it in diction and rhyme. Finally an edited
and approved new version was ready for publication
on April 24, 1881, in the *Montgomery Advertiser*.
The complete poem is as follows:

ALABAMA

Alabama, Alabama,
We will aye be true to thee,
From thy Southern shore where groweth,
By the sea, thy orange tree.
To thy Northern vale where floweth
Deep and blue thy Tennessee.
Alabama, Alabama,
We will aye be true to thee!

Broad the stream whose name thou bearest;
Grand thy Bigbee rolls along;
Fair thy Coosa-Tallapoosa;
Bold thy Warrior, dark and strong;
Goodlier than the land that Moses
Climbed lone Nebo's Mount to see,
Alabama, Alabama,
We will aye be true to thee!

From thy prairies broad and fertile,
Where the snow-white cotton shines,
To the hills where coal and iron
Hide in thy exhaustless mines,
Strong-armed miners—sturdy farmers;
Loyal hearts, whate'er we be,
Alabama, Alabama,
We will aye be true to thee!

From thy quarries where the marble
White as that of Paros gleams,
Waiting till thy sculptor's chisel
Wake to life thy poet's dreams;
For not only wealth of nature,
Wealth of mind hast thou in fee,
Alabama, Alabama,
We will aye be true to thee!

Where the perfumed south-wind whispers,
Thy magnolia groves among,
Softer than a mother's kisses,
Sweeter than a mother's song;
Where the golden jasmine trailing,
Woos the treasure-laden bee,
Alabama, Alabama,
We will aye be true to thee!

Brave and pure thy men and women,
Better this than corn and wine,
Make us worthy, God in Heaven,
Of this goodly land of thine;
Hearts as open as our doorways,
Liberal hands and spirits free,
Alabama, Alabama,
We will aye be true to thee!

Little, little, can I give thee,
Alabama, mother mine;
But that little—hand, brain, spirit—
All I have and am are thine,
Take, O take, the gift and giver,
Take and serve thyself with me,
Alabama, Alabama,
I will aye be true to thee!

In spite of Julia's own preference that her poem
be sung to the tune of the Austrian National An-
them, the same as "Deutschland," this particular air
never caught on. Later, one of her associates suggested the old tune of "Harwell" because of its
familiarity and this was widely used until 1931 when
the Alabama legislature adopted a new musical arrangement.

From the evidence available one can surmise that
the interval from the autumn of 1874 until Julia's
return to the United States in the spring of 1876
was more a period of hard work and privation than
one of pleasure and relaxation. During part of this
time she boarded modestly in Berlin at the home
of a Dr. Mahr, a philologist. During the school year
of 1874-75 she was a teacher in a small German
boarding school run by a Madame Polenz in the
town of Steglitz. Steglitz was a suburb of Berlin,
located on a railroad line about five miles southwest
of the center of the city. Once again, as at Kaiserswerth, the life was plain and strict. In the winter,
there was little or no heat in the bedroom. The
fare was simple and scanty. Julia observed that an
American planter's family generally left more food
on a table when the family had finished than there
was on a German table when the family sat down.
At Madame Polenz' school there was neither tea
nor coffee in the evening, only a kind of soup or
porridge, bread and butter, with ham or sausage

laid upon it. She missed the two kinds of vegetables served at Kaiserswerth; now there was only one, usually potatoes.

In spite of these hardships, she eagerly sought to interest at least one sister, Netta, in a project to recruit a number of American school children to come as boarding students to Madame Polenz' school in Steglitz. Very early in her German sojourn Julia had become strongly convinced that it was a waste of time for an American to begin her study of a modern language in the United States if she subsequently went abroad to study. It is not surprising that as part of her own enthusiastic response to her opportunities she should seek means to bring her sister and her nieces, even her father, over to Europe for a period of study. She made elaborate plans whereby one or more of her relations might get a party of students together and charge fees large enough to provide a sizable surplus. Thus several Tutwiler adults and children might make the trip to Europe and embark on a course of study.

In describing the advantages of study abroad to her hesitant sisters back home at the Greene Springs School, Julia was emphatic in the high estimate she gave to the tangible and intangible values of residence in a foreign country. She believed that even the reputation of having studied abroad was sufficient to enable a woman teacher to secure a well-paying position in the United States with not too many hours of teaching. Even more important, a trip abroad would give a southern woman the cultural stimulation of visiting great cities and of seeing fine paintings and handsome churches. Then, too, there was the enrichment of the mind and the personality. Julia approved of the fact that "people come abroad to get over their national as well as their personal self-conceit and they must take it 'cool & easy.'" She described in some detail just what her sister or, presumably, any similar young woman, might expect to gain from two years of study in Germany. The specific advantages to be secured from such a period of study she listed as follows:

1. a proficiency in the German language
2. the ability to write German in the approved Gothic script
3. an acquaintance with German literature, history, and geography
4. the study of the French language, even though French grammar was studied in close relationship to the German language
5. the opportunity to take music lessons, either instrumental or vocal, especially how to teach vocal music to classes
6. attendance at lectures in the Victoria Lyceum in Berlin on literature, history, or geography.[12]

In spite of these persuasive efforts no relatives came to join Julia in Germany. Like many another

student and tourist, as time drew near for the end
of the sojourn abroad, she expressed some concern
over missed cultural opportunities. There was the
matter of a failure to begin during the first days at
Kaiserswerth a systematic study of German grammar and conversation. She regretted that she had
not attended more of the lectures at the Victoria
Lyceum in Berlin and that she had not visited
theatres and museums more frequently.

During these three years of travel and study
abroad, Julia gave some thought to future plans.
In letters home reference was made to money, honor,
and usefulness in the world as desirable lifetime
goals. Although she believed any woman could
make a good living by translating German books
and articles into English, the career of translator
had little personal appeal. The two professions
Julia seriously considered were writing and teaching. Authorship offered the chance to have one's
ideas made known to others. On the other hand,
to be a successful writer required not only the ex-
penditure of time and energy but also the ability
constantly to project new ideas. After weighing the
pros and cons of the two professions in realistic
fashion, Julia came to the decision that teaching
was the best and most suitable profession for her.
She hoped to find a position in her native South
that would pay her annually a thousand dollars plus
her room and board.[13]

As the time drew near in the spring of 1876 for
Julia to return home, one can only guess at her
thoughts. At a time when opportunities for women
to obtain advanced study were limited in the United
States and in Europe, she had pursued a wide range
of studies. The three German years had been
marked by considerable loneliness and privation
but she had observed German educational methods
and had followed an eclectic course of study with
an emphasis on educational procedures. Few American women of the era had received as thorough a
grounding in teaching methods. Modest and direct
in manner, with realistic awareness of the limita-
tions of her previous schooling, she had found her
training in practical places like the Institute of Deaconesses at Kaiserswerth and in simple surroundings
like the girls' boarding school run by Madame Polenz in Steglitz. Her experiences had broadened
her outlook on the world, deepened her interest in
people, and strengthened her religious sentiment.
She had come to Europe as a tourist and remained
as a student and teacher. She left, a mature and
trained woman, eager to take up once again her
teaching career in her native land.

3. Constructive Pioneer

TEACHER AND ADMINISTRATOR:
1876-1910

WHEN JULIA TUTWILER returned to the United States in 1876 after three years spent in Europe she was 35 years old. Through personal experience she knew the hardships and the sacrifices required if a woman were to gain an education and prepare for a profession. She could look back to the early stimulus and inspiration given her by a loving and encouraging father. She knew the practical side of life, the sharpness and the bitterness of sectional conflict and the burden of rebuilding a new way of life after the War. Her many and varied experiences had developed her capabilities, increased her sympathies, and enlarged her vision. For the remainder of her life, until death in 1916, she was to give herself generously to educational, humanitarian, and reform endeavors.

First of all, there was the task of finding employment. In retrospect, it is understandable that Miss Tutwiler should turn to teaching, because that had been her father's profession and it was the one for which she had prepared herself so conscientiously in America and in Europe during the previous decade. A woman needed courage and confidence in her professional preparation if she sought to enter the higher levels in the teaching profession in the 1870's. By tradition, teaching in formal institutions had been a male prerogative and nowhere had this been more true than in the ante-bellum South. A slow growth in the numbers and the percentage of women teachers had been under way in the United States since the 1830's. Many factors contributed to this gradual increase. One was the adoption, especially in the northeast and in the cities, of the graded school. This educational device made it feasible to place women teachers in charge of the younger pupils while reserving the older boys for the firmer disciplinary control of men teachers. Then, too, during the middle decades of the nineteenth century women benefited from the rapidly increasing educational opportunities. This gave them the necessary background and preparation for teaching. Not to be overlooked were the vastly increased need for teachers, the relative shortage of men especially during and after the war years, and the fact that women would teach for less pay than men. Even so, as late as 1885-86 male teachers still were in the majority in thirteen states, all of which were in the South except Indiana. In that year, only 36 per cent of the teachers in Alabama were women as compared with 40 per cent in North Carolina, 50 per cent in Virginia, and 89 per cent in Massachusetts.[1]

We do not know for certain just what led Julia Tutwiler to embark with zest and purposefulness on a career of teaching in her native state. Quite possibly she felt challenged as a member of the previously privileged class to bear a share in the building of a new South. Like many other gently-bred southern women of the planter aristocracy, she must have felt an impulse to give of herself in the creation of a new way of life. There could be no better way to the future than the one marked by education. And a familiar landmark—the academy—lay ready to hand. Into the revival of the old seminaries of learning for women she threw herself with heart, soul, and mind. In this, a twofold purpose might be accomplished—the preservation of a traditional cultural institution and the establishment of a new device to broaden the outlook and improve the training of the youth of the future.

Nevertheless, while Julia Tutwiler turned with loyalty and affection to the private academy as a

residue of southern educational tradition, she increasingly became aware of the potential importance
of publicly supported educational institutions.

It took faith and perseverance to advocate the
expansion of public education in the South in the
1880's and 1890's. The negative aftereffects of the
Reconstruction period proved to be obstacles to
those who advocated change or reform. The widespread misuse of public funds, the imposition of
heavy taxes, and a rapid increase in bonded debt
served to strengthen the opposition of most southerners to new proposals costing money. Other
factors hindered the improvement of southern educational facilities. Confidence and faith in education
as a basic principle of public welfare had to be
established among the people before any real progress could be made. Then there was the problem
of securing funds for the construction of school
buildings and for the training and the salaries of
teachers. Until the southern people recognized the
fact that their poverty was partly a result of poor
schools, public school education in the South could
advance only very slowly. So many were the difficulties to be overcome that it was not until well
into the twentieth century that a great educational
reawakening occurred in the southern states.

The Alabama to which Julia Tutwiler returned
in the late spring of 1876 was in the final stages of
the re-establishment of home rule. A victory at the

polls by the Democratic Party in 1874 had been followed in 1875 by the adoption of a new state constitution. The last vestiges of Reconstruction were eliminated in 1877 when federal troops were withdrawn from Alabama. Social and economic dislocation and distress remained. Not for many decades were the people of the state able to formulate and adopt workable solutions to their many problems. In this process, Miss Tutwiler was to play an active and influential role.

She entered into a renewal of her earlier professional life by accepting an appointment as a teacher of modern language and English literature at the Tuscaloosa Female College, a Methodist institution chartered in 1859, and located in the small town of Tuscaloosa. Although the school was a young and struggling institution of about 100 students and 10 teachers, it had gained a favorable reputation as one of the leading seminaries for women in Alabama. The level of instruction ranged from the preparatory or primary department through the "regular collegiate" curriculum to the "graduate" department. An extensive offering included traditional primary subjects such as spelling, mental arithmetic, and geography; such classical ones as Latin, Greek, and moral philosophy; and the practical subject of double and single entry bookkeeping. The president was Alonzo Hill, a family friend who had been a former teacher in the Greene Springs School. He voiced his pleasure at securing Julia Tutwiler's services by inserting a notice in the college catalogue that referred to her as a "profound scholar of varied and extended culture . . . an enthusiastic teacher of large and successful experience, [and] . . . one of the most gifted writers of the age."[2]

In these friendly surroundings Miss Tutwiler busied herself from 1876 to 1881 as a teacher of English literature and other subjects. There is little information available about her life during this period and it can only be surmised that she found the teaching interesting but perhaps not overly challenging.

The spark needed to propel her more directly and actively into educational and social affairs came as the inspirational aftermath of a visit to Europe in 1878 to attend the Paris Exposition. Julia Tutwiler had been selected to represent the *National Journal of Education,* a Boston professional publication, and took a leave of absence from her teaching duties to do so. Knowledge of the inspiration and the ideas she gained from this visit comes largely from two articles. Both reports dealt with aspects of the personal and vocational needs of women and foreshadow the future direction of Miss Tutwiler's thought and action.[3]

In one article entitled "The Charities of Paris: What One Woman Can Do," she described in detail the philanthropic activities in Paris of Ada

Leigh, an Englishwoman. Her attention had been
drawn to this woman's work after seeing in the
British section of the Exposition a model representation of one of her charitable projects, a British
orphanage in the Parisian suburb of Neuilly. This
led Miss Tutwiler to make a study of another of
Miss Leigh's welfare activities, a "Mission Home,"
in Paris. In her article Miss Tutwiler described in
detail the circumstances that led to the founding of
this philanthropic center. Miss Leigh's sympathy
and interest had been drawn to the problem of the
welfare of English girls living in Paris. To save them
from various vicissitudes ranging from loneliness to
temptation and degradation, Miss Leigh first insti-
tuted guidance and help based on Bible readings,
religious services and instruction. Subsequently, the
scope of this welfare work had been expanded by
the establishment of a Mission Home where boarding house facilities were available for employed and
unemployed English and American girls. There was
also provision for the special care of the ill. During
the winter a soup kitchen was operated. The staff-
ing was done by volunteer, unpaid "lady helpers."
Here was a practical and positive way, commented
Julia Tutwiler, to provide friendly assistance and
shelter for women unfortunate enough to be without home, friends, or other support. Such whole-
hearted and charitable acceptance of a large share
of responsibility for the moral and physical welfare

of others struck a responsive chord in her generous heart.

In 1880, while she was still a teacher at the Tuscaloosa Female College, Julia drew upon her Paris experiences in a paper she prepared on women's vocational training. At its meeting that year, the Alabama Educational Association heard her views on "The Technical Education of Women." Because it was then deemed "unseemly" for a woman to stand before a large number of men and talk, her address was read by a man. It contained a clearcut description of women's vocational problems and a strong recommendation that vocational training be provided. Such advocacy made Miss Tutwiler one of the very first in America to champion seriously the provision of technical training for women. This paper antedated by several years the establishment of the first state-supported industrial school for women in America and by more than ten years the founding of such a school in Alabama.[4]

In her presentation Julia began by referring to certain nineteenth century population trends in the United States. It was clear to her that eventually most states would have an excess of women over men. She went on to say that although the favored role for a woman was that of wife and mother, still many women, married or single, would have to earn all or part of their living. She then pointed out how limited and poorly paid the range of work was for women, especially in the South. She believed that society as well as the individual was the loser when women were limited for want of training to unskilled and poorly paid jobs. The desirable remedy, she forcefully concluded, was to train women so that they would become true "producers." If women were given a thorough vocational training they would be self-supporting and able to make a direct contribution to the community as well. This thesis shows she was aware of the fact that the existence of low wages and unskilled labor is a disadvantage to the community as well as a handicap to the individual worker.

In the exposition of these ideas on vocational education Miss Tutwiler drew not only on her knowledge of conditions in Alabama and in large areas of the United States but also on her first-hand experiences in various European countries. In France and in Germany she had visited training institutions of the kind she now advocated. In her paper she voiced admiration for the work of Madame Elisa Lemonnier, who had taken the leading part in founding a benevolent society for the vocational training of indigent Parisian girls. This organization in 1862 opened the Ecoles Professionnelles de Jeunes Filles which later served as a model training school for the city of Paris and for the French government. Julia Tutwiler expressed hearty approval of the dual emphasis in this trade school which provided technical and liberal education in a unified course of instruction.

In the elaboration of her ideas Miss Tutwiler displayed a considerable knowledge of the educational scene. She recognized that the expense of establishing a comprehensive program of vocational training for women was too great for current limited resources of private institutions. Resolutely and bravely she stated her conviction that there was an obligation upon the states and the federal government to provide the needed support and direction. She was quick to point out precedents. The federal government had long provided professional military training at West Point and Annapolis. The states had for some time supplied a liberal education and some technical education in the fields of agriculture, mechanic arts, and teaching. But both the federal government and the states had been remiss and backward, she thought, in making fully available to women all the facilities of higher education, academic and vocational. Julia Tutwiler believed that women needed the opportunity for vocational training whether they planned to marry or not. If a woman married after she had some vocational skill she could use that ability to make a better home.

An opportunity to work more actively in the advancement of new educational ideas came in 1881 when Miss Tutwiler was appointed co-principal of the Livingston Female Academy. This academy, located in Livingston, Sumter County, Alabama, had been founded in 1835 by a group of public-spirited people. During the War and Reconstruction years its fortunes had declined until there was fear for its survival. A rebirth began in 1878 with the coming of Carlos G. Smith as principal.[5] He undertook to secure additional financial support, better buildings and equipment, and more pupils. His selection of Julia Tutwiler to be his co-principal met with approval by the trustees and in the community. By now, she was well-known in her own right as an excellent teacher and a person of literary reputation. Moreover she had some distinction as an authority on educational matters. Small wonder, then, that the trustees of the Livingston Female Academy hastened to make public announcement of the new addition to their faculty and administration. In a circular, the Academy officials referred to Miss Tutwiler's "extensive, profound scholarship," her "finished literary taste," and her "distinguished character as a scholar and writer." The expectation was voiced that her many years of experience and her character as a "devoted Christian lady" would enable her to become an "invaluable tutor, exemplar and companion of her pupils."[6]

Julia Tutwiler was an energetic and warm-hearted woman forty years old when she assumed her duties as co-principal of the Livingston Academy in the autumn of 1881. Of medium height and build, it

was her friendly manner and assured bearing that
gave her the ready attention of others. Her hair was
somewhat curly and was dark brown in color. There
was nothing unusual or pretty about her face except
for her keen, alert blue eyes. Many of her contemporaries, however, were particularly struck by her
soft and well-modulated voice. She gave little attention to matters of clothes or style. As the years
passed by, her lack of concern in these matters made
her appear a bit quaint and old-fashioned to some
of her students. In their later reminiscences colleagues and friends alike agreed that unselfishness,
modesty, and seriousness were among her most outstanding characteristics. A warm-hearted, charitable
person, with a strong sense of duty and a rich fund
of knowledge—so did Miss Tutwiler appear to her
students and associates.

It is readily apparent that Julia was an unconven-
tional classroom teacher when measured by the usual
pedagogical standards and procedures of that era.
From her earliest days as a student and teacher under
the supervision of her father she had valued freedom
of subject matter and classroom procedures. Her
experiences at the Institute of Deaconesses at Kaiserswerth and elsewhere in Germany had further
confirmed her dislike of formalized instruction procedures. As she was to point out in her speech in
Toronto in 1891 she disliked pedantic lectures, rote
recitation, and textbook memorization. In her

classes at the Livingston Academy she did not hold herself entirely bound by the curriculum or the specific assignment. In a course in Biblical studies she felt free to discourse at length on the botanical characteristics of some flower she had happened to pick on the way to class. Certain subjects were of special interest to her. As might be expected after many years of residence and study abroad, she liked to teach foreign languages. Quite understandably she was not content with the then current practices in foreign language teaching. She thought that there was usually too much reliance on textbooks and on instruction by Americans who had neither special training nor study abroad. It was her belief that a truly skilled instructor could teach students the basic principles of German in a rapid and intensive course of two months duration.

Two other subjects in the general "collegiate" curriculum were her particular specialties. These were Biblical studies and English literature. In order to develop an appreciation for the classics Miss Tutwiler often dramatized selections by providing a musical arrangement and by making use of oral readings and of a "speech chorus." Her students later credited their excellent knowledge of the Bible and of such authors as Shakespeare, Milton, Tennyson, and Longfellow to her practice of presenting literary materials in both oral and musical settings. She encouraged creative writing and developed the

custom of having the best senior essays read at the
commencement ceremonies.

Two of Miss Tutwiler's unusual qualifications as
an educator were the range and the depth of her
education and the extent of her professional training. From observation and personal experience she
knew how advantageous it was to receive adequate
preparation for a profession. Looking about her she
was depressed by the few vocational opportunities
open to women and by the lack of training available
for those who wanted to teach. As early as 1880 she
publicly expressed her belief that there was an obligation upon state governments to provide literary
and vocational education for women at the college
level. She was also convinced that professional
preparation was needed if school teachers were to
meet and perform their duties adequately. Julia
Tutwiler knew that far too many teachers in Alabama and elsewhere in the United States were lacking in professional training and spirit. Above all
what she wanted to do was to make teaching a true
profession with a formal, publicly financed program
of preparation. This meant the establishment of
institutions designed to train men and women to
become teachers. Publicly supported normal schools
for this purpose had first been provided in the
United States during the 1830's. However it was
not until well after the War that this type of vocational institution became widespread. At first it was

customary for state legislatures to provide subsidies to private schools for the particular purpose of giving some training to would-be teachers. Missouri and Alabama were the leaders among the southern states in this important public school development.

The first real opportunity for Julia Tutwiler to put into practice her strongly held theory that school teachers should receive professional training came in 1883. It was in this year that the Alabama legislature authorized an annual appropriation of $2,500 to establish a normal school department in the Livingston Academy. In this manner the state partially met its obligation to prepare teachers for the public schools of Alabama. There was ample precedent for this method both in the country at large and in Alabama. During the carpetbag period, in 1870 and 1871, the Alabama legislature had established normal schools for the training of Negro teachers and white teachers. The arrangement between the state and the Livingston Academy was that the latter should establish and operate the Alabama Normal College for Girls at Livingston as a branch of the Academy. In return for the yearly subsidy ($2,000 was allotted for instructional costs and $500 for equipment) the Academy was to furnish teachers and instruction to train young women to teach in Alabama's public schools. A major share of credit for this significant expansion in the functions and the financial resources of the Livingston Academy

must go to Julia Tutwiler herself. For some time
she had ardently advocated state financial support
for the training of public school teachers.

With this grant of state funds to establish a teacher
training program the Livingston Academy began to
develop an expanded curriculum. Changes were
made, effective in the academic year 1883-84, to free
Miss Tutwiler for most of this work. In addition to
the two co-principals there was a teaching staff of
eight others (all women) to carry the teaching load
of a curriculum ranging from the primary division
up to a so-called collegiate department. Julia Tutwiler was listed as teaching four of the subjects in the collegiate department: Literature,
German, Mental and Moral Philosophy, and Normal Methods.

The requirements of admission to the new normal training course, listed in the 1883-84 *Livingston
Academy Catalogue,* included the following:

  (1) applicants had to be at least fourteen years
      old and it was preferred that they be older
      than that;
  (2) pupils under eighteen years of age were
      not permitted to board in town except in
      the home of the Principal or a near relative;
  (3) applicants had to pass an entrance examina-
      tion in arithmetic, English grammar, and
      the geography and history of the United
      States, with a grade qualifying them to ad-

mission to the first year of the collegiate course;

(4) each applicant had to sign a written statement of intention to complete the teacher course and to teach for at least two years in Alabama.

The catalogue stated that students in the new teacher training program had a choice of either a short or a long program. Those in the short two-year course were to receive a teaching certificate only. The completion of the full four-year curriculum would mean the attainment of a diploma as well as a teaching certificate. At this time and until 1901 graduates of certain normal schools, Livingston included, automatically upon graduation received teaching certificates without further examination. In both the short and the long course, the catalogue went on to say, there would be instruction in teaching methods and the provision of practice teaching in the final year. All students in the normal department were expected to elect subjects in the regular collegiate department as well. Tuition was free for normal school students.

Thus at the very outset of her long and distinguished career as an administrator Julia Tutwiler was largely responsible for the development of a comprehensive program for the training of public school teachers. It included such progressive features as

(1) a test of academic fitness as a prerequisite
     for admission to the normal school course
(2) professional training in education methods
(3) practice teaching under supervision
(4) emphasis on the continued and advanced
     study of liberal arts subjects.

It is true enough that during the period of Miss
Tutwiler's lifetime the work of the normal schools
in Alabama rarely if ever exceeded a twelve-year
program. In fact, most of the work of the normal
schools was distinctly on the secondary level.[7] Yet
credit must be given to her for recognizing the need
to define standards and to work towards their attainment. Of course the entrance requirements of
the Livingston Academy and its normal school had
to be geared to the rather limited level of attainment
of the graduates of the lower schools of Alabama in
the last decades of the nineteenth century. Indeed,
throughout the United States at this period the academic standards of most normal schools were on a
par with those of the high schools. As late as 1890
there were only a few city teacher training institutions that could require graduation from high
school as an entrance prerequisite.

In the 1880's the town of Livingston had approximately 800 inhabitants, a small population to
support an academy and normal school. And so
Julia Tutwiler early began the practice of traveling
about the state to interest girls in coming to Living-

JULIA TUTWILER (CENTER) AND LIVINGSTON FACULTY

JULIA TUTWILER HALL, LIVINGSTON STATE COLLEGE

JULIA TUTWILER HALL, ALABAMA COLLEGE

JULIA TUTWILER HALL, UNIVERSITY OF ALABAMA

ston for their education. As she drove along the dusty roads in her buggy, she was alert to possible candidates for her school. There is on record her success in inducing at least one young boy to come and take up his studies at Livingston.[8]

In order to provide housing for the out-of-town students, Miss Tutwiler used her own funds to buy land adjoining the Academy grounds. Here she erected cottages to house and board these students. In this manner by her own initiative and investment she made possible a slow growth in the number of students.

As time passed, changes in the relative importance of the functions of the Livingston Academy led to a somewhat confusing series of modifications in the name of the institution. Nor were the changes always consistently followed thereafter. In the 1893-94 issue of the school's catalogue there was no reference to the Academy and the name Alabama Normal College for Girls was used. This was often shortened to "A.N.C." Sometimes a combination of place and function was effected in the use of the name "Livingston Normal College." It is quite true that this institution in Julia Tutwiler's lifetime remained a normal school and was not a true college in the modern sense. The continuing variations in the name of the institution give testimony to the educational developments under way during these decades.

The death of Henry Tutwiler on September 24,

1884, by severing the closest tie with the family home at Greene Springs, left Julia Tutwiler freer to concentrate on her career and special interests. Energetically she endeavored to raise the standards and advance the prestige of her institution. She would have liked to reach the levels set by public normal colleges in the nation's large cities. But she was a practical woman as well as one of vision. She recognized that she had to begin with the situation as it was and to be content with a curriculum and admission standards adjusted to fit the educational situation of rural Alabama. Therefore it continued to be the practice at Livingston, for example, for special courses to be offered at all levels to provide students with the necessary fundamentals in subject-matter fields. Furthermore, the students had several choices as to length and difficulty of their course of instruction. Every effort was made to adjust the instruction to meet the level of previous preparation and the particular needs and ambitions of the individual student.

One can only sketch the nature and content of the normal school program from the printed notices in the school's catalogues. Normal school students were required to have a set of the readers and spellers of William McGuffey from the primer through the sixth reader. In the list of texts and reference books the following authors were given: Henry Barnard, Friedrich Froebel, David Page,

Francis Wayland Parker, and William Harold Payne.

Other aspects of the normal school curriculum at Livingston deserve particular description. Special or "eclectic" courses continued to be available to those students who desired additional training. Further, Miss Tutwiler expanded the course of study and developed instructional methods so that students would have a greater interest in and understanding of the subjects they were studying. Two of the methods she used will be most readily identified in their present-day terms: visual aids and field trips. Her use of the technique of visual instruction is seen in the provision of such scientific apparatus as a telescope, a microscope, an air pump, an electric-magnetic battery, and examples of the incandescent and arc lights. She was active in adding natural science items to the "Cabinet" or collection used in the teaching of geology, botany, physiology, zoölogy, and astronomy.

Another feature, unusual for the period, was the use of supervised school trips as a device for giving the students a first-hand opportunity to see places of historic and cultural interest. During the winter of 1881-82 the first of these school excursions was made to the exposition in Atlanta. Subsequently, other places were visited. In May of 1887, a large group of students and friends of the school went on a tour to Washington, D. C., and visited museums, art collections, and public buildings under Miss Tutwiler's guidance. The cost to each pupil for the excursion was $25.00.

Changes took place also in the administration of the Livingston Normal College. In 1888 Dr. Carlos Smith resigned from the co-principalship because of age and poor health. For two years from 1888 to 1890 Captain J. W. A. Wright, one of Miss Tutwiler's brothers-in-law, served with her in the position. In 1890 the Livingston trustees made Julia Tutwiler the president and sole principal, a post she filled until her retirement in 1910.

Meanwhile the academy and the normal school were growing slowly but steadily in numbers of students and in prestige. By 1888 there were 126 students in attendance, of whom 37 were normal school pupils. In one of the contemporary guides to Alabama, Livingston was cited as the possessor of a fine normal school "of great repute, and conducted by educators of distinction."[9]

Some indication of Julia Tutwiler's growing stature as an educator in her native state and in the country may be seen in the record of her participation in the National Educational Association. At the 1884 meeting of the Association in Madison, Wisconsin, she was elected one of the national "counsellors" of the organization for a two-year term.[10] The minutes of the 1886 session do not indicate positively whether she was active as a board member during the meeting of that year, held in Topeka,

Kansas.[11] In July, 1890, at the St. Paul meeting of the NEA, when she gave her first paper before a national audience, she stated that this was the fifth convention of the NEA that she had attended.[12] It can reasonably be assumed that one of these was the 1884 meeting at Madison when she had been nominated and elected as a "counsellor" or member of the board of directors. Although the records are not specific on the point, it is likely that she was also present at three of these conventions: in 1885 at Saratoga Springs, New York; in 1886 at Topeka, Kansas; in 1887 at Chicago, Illinois; in 1888 at San Francisco, California; and in 1889 at Nashville, Tennessee.

The subject she chose for her speech at the 1891 convention in Toronto, Canada, "A Year in a German Model School," was a most appropriate topic in an era when the ideas of Pestalozzi, Froebel, and Herbart were at their greatest vogue in American educational circles. At this session of the NEA, she was elected to the position of president of the Department of Elementary Education, a post that carried with it automatic membership on the Association's Board of Directors. This election was a noteworthy recognition of her interest and participation in national educational affairs.[13]

In 1892, at the NEA meeting in Saratoga Springs, New York, Julia Tutwiler as president presided over the section meetings of the Department of Elementary Education. She spoke briefly on the topic of "Individualization by Grouping." She believed there were two distinct natures in each child: the spiritual and emotional side and the physical and intellectual. It was important, she thought, to attempt to meet individual differences and needs in boys and girls. Children varied in their ability to draw, to write, to use music, and to figure. Why not, she asked, try an experiment? For the first two primary grades, separate children according to their ability and proficiency in the four areas of music, art, literature, and mathematics. Then give special, advanced instruction in the particular fields of greatest interest and ability. In this way, Miss Tutwiler argued, there would be an early opportunity to recognize and encourage the boy or girl with special talent.[14]

During the Columbian World's Fair in Chicago in the summer of 1893, Julia Tutwiler participated actively in at least three of the associated cultural congresses. She served as one of Alabama's three honorary vice-presidents to the International Congress of Education. She attended the International Historical Congress of Charities and Corrections and presented a report on the status of charitable and humanitarian activity in Alabama. Thirdly, she was one of the group of about 330 noted women from all parts of the world who were invited to participate in the World's Congress of Representative

Women. The topic that she discussed in the Assembly Hall of the Women's Building was "Is Self Support Possible for Girls During the Years of Secondary Education?"[15]

On this important occasion before a noted international audience, Julia Tutwiler grappled with a problem of growing importance—how to assist needy students to further their education. In her opinion it was unwise to try to combine employment and study at the same time. She believed that there was sufficient physical and mental activity in school work to preclude the advisability of doubling the load by adding the strains associated with part-time work. But what about the poor girl, she asked, who could not afford to attend high school or college unless she received financial help outside her family? Job opportunities were few for her, particularly in rural areas, and never well-paid. Julia Tutwiler's solution for this problem was unusual and ingenious. She advocated the establishment by the school of an industrial enterprise, like canning, in its own buildings. The needy student would be given her board and room and employed during the summer months in this college-run factory. All wages earned were to be withheld and credited to board and tuition in the regular academic year. As a further advantage to her plan, Miss Tutwiler cited the fact that it would make use of college buildings otherwise vacant during the summer vacation. She concluded her talk by expressing her conviction that her idea was economically feasible. Certainly this proposal does credit to her warmth of heart and her inventiveness even if it leaves the present-day reader with some uneasy doubt as to its financial practicality.[16]

As the years progressed Miss Tutwiler did not lose her interest in travel nor her appreciation of the value of study. Unfortunately, although we know she made several trips to Europe during these middle years of her life, details are lacking.[17] An important national and sectional educational and religious activity in which she participated was the Chautauqua movement. The basic purpose of this organization was to provide adults with education and with spiritual inspiration in a voluntary group experience. Although the movement had a strongly religious character, it was not narrow or sectarian in outlook. Many Americans in the latter decades of the nineteenth century seized upon the Chautauqua movement as an opportunity to use their increased leisure time profitably to improve on an earlier, and often inadequate, educational background. The original Chautauqua Assembly expanded rapidly. Summer schools and home reading circles were established in many other localities.[18]

In 1882 a summer conference for Sunday school workers was organized by a group of southern religious leaders in the little town of Monteagle, in the Cumberland Mountains of Tennessee. This town had long been known as a healthful summer resort for those seeking to escape the summer heat and epidemics of southern cities. In 1883 this religious conference became a Chautauqua Assembly, lasting eight weeks during the summer. Apparently Julia Tutwiler was among the very first members, for she began her association with this assembly in 1883. By 1885 she had built a house there and had become a permanent member of the faculty. Subsequently, she erected a number of cottages at Monteagle for the use during the summer of her family, colleagues, and students. Thus she participated as a teacher and leader for many years in one of the earliest and most successful of the attempts to bring adult education to the American people.[19]

The extent and significance of Julia Tutwiler's activities in both Alabama and the nation accounts for her inclusion in a volume of biographical sketches of 1,470 eminent American women published in 1893.[20] She was then 52 years old. Her many outside interests in no way lessened her participation in the growth and development of the Academy and normal school at Livingston.

One of her continuing duties was to encourage qualified girls to enter the teacher training course. In the summer months, she traveled through the rural sections of the state seeking applicants. When she found an ambitious girl who needed help in paying her board and other expenses, she sought

loan funds[21] or, if necessary, lent money herself.
Miss Tutwiler was known as a person who would
never say "no" to a poor girl who wanted an education. Her generosity was described as follows:

> Not one of the hundreds of girls in straitened cir-
> cumstances who have come to her for an education has
> ever been turned away, great-hearted woman that she is!
> If her pocket happened to be empty at the moment, she
> always discovered someone with means to assist those eager,
> ambitious girls. Julia Tutwiler, you see, is the kind of
> woman whose hand is always going down into her pocket
> to help someone or some cause.
> Is Julia Tutwiler rich, then, that she can spend so freely?
> Oh, no! How could that be with such a nature? She would
> laugh if she heard you. The only luxury this busy, generous
> woman lives in is the luxury of giving and serving.[22]

The Livingston Normal College students had good
reason, therefore, to remember the sympathy and
open-handedness with which their beloved president
responded to their needs.

Julia Tutwiler busied herself also with the larger
task of finding adequate income for the Academy
and the normal school. The problem was to secure
sufficient funds to meet the expenses of the institution and yet not place tuition and boarding fees so
high as to discourage attendance. During most of
her twenty-nine-year tenure, the subsidy from the
state and the contributions from private benefactors
and trustees of the semi-public Academy were modest in amount. Therefore, in order to provide for

physical growth and to expand the curriculum, she was led to adopt fiscal practices of generous intent but doubtful wisdom. She used her own salary and personal funds to rent, equip, and operate private buildings as dormitories and dining halls for the housing and boarding of students. Much of the net income from her boarding department she then put into operating funds for the academic budget.[23] This intermingling of her own personal funds with those obtained from state subsidies, student fees, and private philanthropic contributions may have helped in the early growth of the institution. As a permanent practice, however, such a policy was bound to create misunderstanding and friction when the budget of the normal school later came under direct surveillance by state authorities.

Late in December, 1894, a temporary disaster befell the institution. A fire destroyed the college building. Subsequently in the next year, two new buildings were constructed at a cost of $7,000. The academic structure contained fourteen rooms and the dormitory twenty-eight.[24]

During the decade of the 1890's at least two significant additions were made to the offerings of the Livingston Normal College. These were the introduction of a kindergarten department and the inauguration of vocational training. The catalogue for the year 1896-97 contained the announcement that a kindergarten would be opened. In Septem-

ber 1898 a total of 74 pupils was reported as
enrolled. In the recruitment of pupils for the kindergarten Miss Tutwiler employed the form of direct solicitation she had used so characteristically
and effectively for the normal school. One very
young boy was encouraged in 1910 to come to the
kindergarten by her offer of an ice cream soda.[25]

The vocational subjects listed to be taught in the
Academy, effective with the 1896-97 session, included printing, dress cutting and fitting, type-
writing and shorthand, bookkeeping, and telegraphy.
In view of the modest population of the town of
Livingston and the already extended curriculum in
terms of financial resources and faculty, the wisdom
of these additions may be questioned. It may well
be that Julia Tutwiler believed it was incumbent
upon her to do what she could, thin though the
preparation must have been, to meet the vocational
needs of girls who could not prepare to be teachers
but who needed employment.

A far clearer and more significant academic distinction for Livingston Normal College came in
1899 when it was added by the University of Alabama to the list of University Auxiliary Schools.
This meant that the Livingston course of study met
the entrance standards of the University. Henceforth, Livingston graduates were admitted to the
University of Alabama by certificate, without an
entrance examination.

As the years passed by, Julia Tutwiler continued to have the respect and admiration of her students for her wide range of knowledge and her nationally recognized attainments as an educator. More and more, however, it was her selfless character and her generous interest in them that they valued the most. One of her most endearing qualities was a warm-hearted sympathy. It was at her morning chapel talks that she particularly exerted a personal influence on the student body. These "were heart to heart revelations to all, and made each girl feel inspired to do her best and win the approval of this great 'Mother of them all.' "[26]

Immersed though she was in Livingston and its students, Miss Tutwiler increasingly felt that Livingston problems were eventually part of a greater whole—the building of an adequate system of education in Alabama. At the turn of the century, several progressive steps were widely believed to be necessary if public school education in Alabama was ever to be worthy of the term "modern." At least three needs were to receive emphasis: (1) greater financial support for all the state public schools; (2) a more effective system of state supervision; and (3) the employment of better teachers. For the first time, a trained and experienced educator, John W. Abercrombie, became state superintendent of education. Among the measures that he strongly recommended were two that directly affected the

Livingston Normal College. One of these was an
increase in the yearly state subsidy, from $2,500 to
$7,500, effective in 1901-02. The other was the en-
actment in 1899 of a law that placed the examination and certification of all public school teachers
in the hands of a state board of examiners. This last
reform had long been advocated as a means of elimi-
nating the low standards, inefficiency, and politics
of duplicate county and city certification. Under
the new act, there were three separate levels of certification. A "third grade" certificate was good for
two years and was not renewable. A "second grade"
certificate was valid for four years and could be
renewed once. The "first grade" and life certificates
were based on examinations in secondary school
subjects as well as those of the elementary school.
Thus teachers were forced to improve their knowledge or leave the profession.

The certification of teachers by the State Board
of Examiners, beginning in 1899-1900, ended the
privilege hitherto enjoyed by the state's normal
schools of granting state certificates to their graduates. The new law had the effect of placing a
responsibility on the normal schools to prepare their
students to pass the state examination. It would appear that Julia Tutwiler had earlier endorsed the
idea of uniform teacher certification. Sometime
prior to 1899, under the pen name of "Mother
Alabama," she had circulated a broadside to the

members of the Alabama legislature advocating, among other measures, the adoption of a state system of teacher certification.[27]

Adoption of certification by examination was, of course, primarily designed to eliminate unqualified persons from the profession. In 1899-1900, the first year of operation under the new plan, approximately 4,000 applicants, or forty per cent of those taking the examinations, were unsuccessful. Those who wished to teach now found it profitable to take formal training before trying to pass the certification examination. Thus the new procedures had the effect of taxing the teaching resources of the normal schools. A great many young women made application to the Livingston Normal College for the purpose of receiving what, in actual practice, was a form of tutoring. Practical educator that she was, Miss Tutwiler at once devoted her efforts to the preparation of students for these examinations. The Livingston Normal College catalogue of 1902-03 lists the following "pedagogies" as included in the second, third, and final years of the four year "collegiate course": pedagogy, elocution, psychology, history of education, school of teachers, school law of Alabama and practice teaching. She also proposed to a former student and colleague, apparently without success, that the two of them write a question-and-answer review manual.[28]

Although Miss Tutwiler endeavored with considerable success to prepare her students to pass the state teacher examinations, she also deplored the fact that the specificity of the new system encouraged the practice of cramming. She was fearful lest the enumeration of twelve designated subjects for the most advanced certificate would cause other worthwhile subjects (like English literature, Latin, or calisthenics) to be overlooked. She warned of the danger in "an influx of teachers who are well acquainted with a certain number of textbooks on a limited number of subjects, but without that indefinable essence called 'culture.' "[29]

The annual report of the Livingston Normal College for the year 1903-04 indicates that students from 40 of the 67 counties of the state were in residence. There were eight graduates in the normal school, four in the literary department, and one in art. For the period from 1883 to 1904, it was reported that the total number of graduates from the normal department was 210, and from the literary department, 73. In pleasing contrast to the many long years when her stipend was approximately $500, Julia Tutwiler's salary as president and professor of Latin, Greek, French, German, and Spanish was listed as $2,250. The state subsidy was $10,000, an increase of $2,500 over what it had been in 1901-02. The board and room fee, on a nine months' basis and including laundry and medical charges, was $108.[30]

In Alabama, during the nineteenth century, there

ENTRANCE TO JULIA TUTWILER PRISON, WETUMPKA

JULIA S. TUTWILER BRIDGE AT GAINESVILLE

JULIA TUTWILER AS LIVINGSTON COLLEGE PRESIDENT

had been little or no interest among the many small and competing private and public schools, academies, and colleges in preventing unnecessary duplication of effort. In general, it was true that the low admission standards of the colleges had the effect of preventing the growth of a true system of secondary education. After 1900, progressive educators in the state joined in a movement to raise the level of college entrance requirements and thus encourage the growth of high schools. In June, 1908, the presidents of eight colleges and normal schools founded an organization known as the Association of Alabama Colleges. Three of the normal schools, including the Livingston Normal College, were among the original members. One of the immediate projects of the Association was to work towards the adoption in Alabama of a college admission requirement at the level of fourteen Carnegie units of high school work.[31]

From fragmentary evidence available it is apparent that Julia Tutwiler through participation in such educational gatherings as the Conference for Education in the South[32] had become convinced of the desirability of raising college admission standards. While attending an otherwise not identified "Conference of Southern Educators" sometime during the first decade of the twentieth century, she kept some notes on a conference session devoted to the question "Are Southern Schools Ready to Meet the Requirement of Fourteen Units for Admission to College?" She was favorably impressed by the account given by a professor from the University of Texas of the success of that institution in gradually raising the level from eight to eleven units, with "conditions" in three others. She was realistic enough to include in her notes the observation that colleges must not raise their entrance requirements above the level of attainment of the high school.[33]

The early years of the twentieth century brought additional educational changes in Alabama. A new state constitution, in effect by November of 1901, contained many provisions to stimulate the development of a better system of public education. New laws were passed to increase the funds available for the schools, to lengthen the school term, and to provide for greater uniformity and state supervision. As part of this process of expansion and of standardization, the supervision and direction of the state's white normal schools was placed under a central state board of trustees. One of the specific functions of this board was to enforce uniformity in the administration and curriculum of the normal schools. A new era of professionalization of education and extension of facilities was at last opening in Alabama. Pioneering days were over.

During her long career as teacher and administrator, Julia Tutwiler had been more of a pioneer than a conformer. Many of her most notable educational and reform accomplishments had come as a result of her own direct and personal action. She had had little experience working for anyone outside of a family relationship. Although she had done much to extend public educational opportunities for women, she was not prepared by nature or by training to fit herself easily into a state system of education. Essentially a sensitive, impulsive woman of deep convictions, Julia Tutwiler could not, in the last years of her life, readily adapt herself to new administrative procedures. Nor did she find it possible to get the financial accounts of the Livingston college into such form as to be satisfactory to the state authorities and to herself.

Early in 1907, in order not to lose the state subsidy, it was necessary to reorganize the Livingston Normal College and to eliminate the local, or private, element of ownership and to transfer all control and property to the state.[34] Previously, the trustees had been Livingston residents and most of them had been members of the Presbyterian Church.[35] By April, Governor B. B. Comer had appointed the first state board for Livingston Normal College. It consisted of two men from the town of Livingston; four from the congressional district; H. C. Gunnels, state superintendent of education; Julia Tutwiler, *ex officio* as president of the school; and the Governor. At the first meeting of the new board of trustees, on April 16, 1907, it was evident that the Governor and the state superintendent of education wanted to centralize and systematize fiscal and personnel policies and practices. The Governor, as president of the board of trustees, appointed committees on rules and regulations of the board; faculty and course of study; buildings and grounds; audits. He named himself, the state superintendent and one lay trustee members of an executive committee to "have general supervision of the school" and to have power "to act on all questions affecting the school when this board is not in session."[36]

The completion of the change-over in ownership and direction from local hands to the state proved to be difficult and contentious. This was in part due to the school's indebtedness. A complex problem was the adjudication of Julia Tutwiler's personal claims of money due her.[37] Following the establishment of state control in 1907, she carried on a considerable correspondence with the Governor and with members of the board of trustees in an effort to clear the accounts, particularly those of the boarding department. For many years, she had run the dormitories and the dining hall almost as a private venture. Her purpose, however, had not been to make money for herself but to house students who could not otherwise attend the normal school. Any profits went, she stated, to pay salaries and to improve the school. This was at a time when the Livingston board of trustees was unwilling to enter into capital outlay projects and the state allocated funds only for tuition and equipment. The accounts had been poorly kept and this contributed further to misunderstanding and friction. Miss Tutwiler had been so unwise, for example, as to advance building rents out of her personal funds, while expecting to be repaid later out of boarders' fees collected by the business manager, who received a state salary. This open-handed, generous use of private and public funds won Julia Tutwiler the devoted love of her students and many Livingston people. It did not, however, endear her, a determined woman of 66 years, to the state officials. The controversy became so involved that far from being a creditor at one point, in July, 1908, it appeared that she owed the state a sum of about $1,300.[38]

It is not clear just how the financial difficulties between Julia Tutwiler and the state board of trustees were eventually settled. As late as May, 1909, the minutes of the trustees refer to her still pending claims for a balance of $1,300 due "for advances made by her as rent for four year [*sic*] on the Dormitory." The minutes of the next annual meeting, in 1910, record that she made an "extended statement" concerning this $1,300 claim. Whereupon the board adopted a resolution which accepted her "voluntary release" of the alleged claim. The board further recorded its conviction that she had erroneously but sincerely believed her claim just.[39]

Meanwhile, this lengthy conflict over financial matters tended to cloud the serenity of Miss Tutwiler's last years at Livingston. In view of her own candid statements of the informal way in which she handled money matters and a board report that the school buildings were in need of repairs, it is understandable that the new board made haste to appoint an experienced man to handle the institution's financial affairs. The new appointee, George W. Brock, took up his duties on July 1, 1907, as professor of ancient languages and mathematics and as administrative assistant to Julia Tutwiler. From the very first, his duties were comprehensive and tended to overlap Miss Tutwiler's as president. Brock's position was originally listed as "secretary of the faculty." He was particularly charged with the collection of "all fees levied on pupils no matter for what purpose." Miss Tutwiler and Brock were made co-equal in recommending curricular changes to the board for final action. In the next year, 1908, the board ruled that Miss Tutwiler and Brock were to share the authority to make recommendations to the board concerning faculty appointments. Discipline of the students was to be handled by the two. Responsibility for the operation of the boarding department was also placed by the board in their joint control. Brock's title was changed to chairman of the faculty.[40]

After his arrival at the college in July of 1907,

Brock energetically—and perhaps none too tactfully —set about his duties. He regarded himself as obligated to see to the repair and the improvement of the college buildings and grounds. Julia Tutwiler, as a member of an older generation less familiar with such conveniences as inside toilets and running water, had perhaps too long neglected the physical plant. Brock, therefore, found the college buildings and equipment old-fashioned and in poor condition. He reported that all of the buildings were dirty and that the dormitories were in need of new furniture. Sanitary conditions Brock found to be most unsatisfactory due to the absence of any system of sewerage or water works. He stated that the rooms and halls were lighted by kerosene lamps; there were no screens at the windows or doors; and the stall of the college horse was located about ten feet from the college dining hall and kitchen.[41]

No doubt such conditions characterized the homes at that time of many residents of small towns and rural areas in Alabama. Indeed, Brock's efforts to improve the grounds and the buildings and to install modern equipment subjected him to considerable adverse comment among the Livingston inhabitants. Like Julia Tutwiler herself, many of them liked the "old ways" and tended to resent his criticisms and the accompanying implication that the prized and revered local institution was not all that it might be. It was hard, too, for Julia Tutwiler and her colleagues and fellow townspeople to become accustomed to her reduced status as a co-president. Perhaps it is true that no one, let alone a spirited, individualistic and distinguished person like Julia Tutwiler, is ever prepared to face objectively the prospect of retirement.

As early as April of 1907, just before Brock's appointment as administrative assistant and business manager, Julia Tutwiler wrote Governor Comer of her fear of being superseded as president of the normal school. She told the Governor of her brother-in-law's forecast that she had "created here something far too good for a woman, and that some man will now kick me out." She went on to say:

I am carrying on plans which I believe will result in great good for great numbers and I should like to be permitted to carry them out to the end. I am trying to make of every student who leaves the school a missionary of Christianity and culture. I send to each one when she begins to teach, a wall copy of the Lord's Prayer, the Creed, and the Ten Commandments, and they promise to teach these to their pupils. . . .

I know that no school in the South is doing more to enlighten the darkness and remove the blot of illiteracy from Alabama than this school.[42]

The decision of the board of trustees of the Normal College to retire Julia Tutwiler from the presidency was made on May 26, 1910, at the same session at which the board had politely but finally rejected one of her long-pending claims against the state. Miss Tutwiler was now nearing her sixty-ninth birthday and had completed 29 years of service as a teacher and administrator in the Livingston school. She had found it a small, semi-private girls' academy and she left it an established and respected state normal school. The board sought to recognize her achievements by electing her to the post of president emeritus and by voting her a monthly salary of $100. The board's resolution was as follows:

That in sincere recognition of the long and successful work of Miss Julia S. Tutwiler for education in Alabama, and more especially her work for Alabama girls, and of her long years of labor in upbuilding this college and in appreciation of her active and continued interest in the upbuilding of the Alabama Normal College,—the position of President-Emeritus of this Institution is now created in her honor, without duties or responsibilities of any character,— this being the first time such position has ever been created in honor of any Alabama educator; that the salary of the President-Emeritus be fixed at one hundred dollars per month; that Miss Tutwiler be and is hereby elected President-Emeritus of Alabama Normal College.[43]

The news of Julia Tutwiler's retirement from the presidency of the normal school received, of course, wide publicity. The granting of a pension to her was favorably commented upon as a most suitable award for her contributions. The idea gained acceptance that this was a pension for life, though such had not been clearly stated in the board's resolution. At the same meeting, the board had elected George W. Brock president of the normal school at an annual salary of $2,250, the same sum previously paid to Julia Tutwiler as president.

Within a day or two after the board's action, one of Julia Tutwiler's associates began a "protest campaign" against the decision of the trustees to retire the noted woman educator. Printed forms were circulated with the request that they be returned to Miss J. Nicholene Bishop, one of Miss Tutwiler's closest friends. This sheet read as follows:

You have doubtless seen in the papers the action of the Board of Trustees in regard to Miss Julia Tutwiler at their last meeting. She has been removed from the position of President and Mr. Brock elected in her place. The statement in the paper sounds very well, but I know personally that she has been accused falsely, and subjected to the greatest indignities.

Will you join us in a protest against such unjust treatment? If so sign the following statement:

We resent for Miss Julia Tutwiler and for the State the recent action of the Board of Trustees:

Just what Miss Bishop hoped to gain by this protest is not evident. When one of Miss Tutwiler's sisters, Mrs. T. C. McCorvey, saw the circular, she wrote to Miss Bishop somewhat in criticism of this effort to retain her sister in her old position as president. Mrs. McCorvey observed sagaciously:

. . . I read the newspaper statement again, and find that "for life" is *not* embodied in their resolution, still I am sure it *will* be for life if sister J. does not act or talk impudently and criticize the head. I fear any protest will only irritate the trustees, and make them withdraw what they have done. . . .

I know this is hard for her to bear, but she ought to take it philosophically. She is now 70 years old, few people can continue in service after that time. From my standpoint she should be thoroughly satisfied with the terms of the retirement if it is for life.

I cannot understand why she would be willing to stay a day in the school where there is so much friction.[44]

Developments of the year 1910-11 were of a nature to cause the trustees of the normal school to discontinue Julia Tutwiler's pension after the first year. Perhaps the views of President Brock that she had ample financial resources and that the money could be used to better advantage by the institution were the determining factors. So it was that after 29 years of service as a teacher and administrator in the Livingston Academy and normal school Miss Tutwiler at 70 had no continuing pension.[45]

Even in the midst of the controversies of her last years at Livingston there had been pleasant occasions that brought a positive sense of warmth and accomplishment to Miss Tutwiler. One of these was in 1906, her twenty-fifth anniversary at Livingston, when the board gave her a silver loving cup. Again, in the spring of 1907, the University of Alabama awarded her an honorary doctorate in recognition of her work in furthering public education in Alabama. At the commencement ceremonies at Liv-

ingston, in 1910, just after the announcement of her
retirement, the alumnae presented her with a silver
loving cup and gave her portrait to the college. The
newspaper account of the unveiling of the picture
stated that the audience rose to its feet and "wildly
cheered" Miss Tutwiler. It continued:

It was a touching scene and many eyes were wet. Miss
Tutwiler's long association with the college has always
made the two seem one and the loyal alumni who have
gone forth each year from the college halls will always
associate Miss Julia with the best of college life. She is the
embodiment of the Alabama Normal College to thousands
of loyal friends throughout the state and they will wish
her many happy years and the richest blessings that can
crown a long and useful career.[46]

It was indeed true that Miss Tutwiler had rounded
out a long and distinguished career as an educator.
This stretched back to her early twenties when during the war years she had taught in her father's
Greene Springs School. Then had followed three
years as teacher and administrator at the Greensboro Academy in Greensboro, Alabama, from 1866
to 1869. Her next formal teaching post had been at
the Tuscaloosa Female College, where she served on
the faculty from 1876 to 1881. It was during her
long service at Livingston Normal College as an administrator and teacher that Julia Tutwiler made
many of her most significant educational contributions. She worked unceasingly to preserve and
strengthen the Academy as a traditional southern

cultural institution. At the same time, she was ahead of most of her southern contemporaries in advocating professional training for teachers and the financing of such training by the state. A major share of the credit for the transformation of the Livingston Academy into a state normal school must go to her. Nor did she overlook the need to work for the improvement of the curriculum and entrance standards and the adoption of statewide teacher certification requirements. Her early emphasis on the value of field trips to various parts of the United States as a means of giving the students a greater interest in subject matter shows another side of her exploring, progressive mind.

In still another way did Miss Tutwiler point out to the people of Alabama new directions in education. As early as 1880 she was publicly advocating vocational education for women. She argued that the provision of such training would not only have a direct economic benefit in making women more efficient producers but it would have desirable cultural benefits as well by making them better citizens and mothers.

In a way rather unusual for a woman in the South in the latter part of the nineteenth century, Miss Tutwiler's achievements in education received national recognition. Most noteworthy perhaps were her services in the National Educational Association. From 1884 to 1886 she was a member of the

national board, and in 1891-92 she was president of
the department of elementary education and also a
member of the board of directors.

Julia Tutwiler's distinguished work as an educator was only a part of her contributions to the
people of Alabama. Although she was busy as a
teacher and an administrator she found the time to
engage in a wide range of additional educational
and humanitarian endeavors. These provide an inspiring story of her activity as a reformer.

4. Ardent Spirit

REFORMER AND HUMANITARIAN:
1880-1910

THROUGHOUT HER LIFE Julia Tutwiler devoted herself to a wide range of reform and humanitarian endeavors. Her concern for the welfare of others grew directly out of her personal convictions and experiences. Her contemporaries believed that her most enduring accomplishments lay in these reform activities. As a determined fighter against ignorance, inhumanity, and evil she was acclaimed as "the purest figure in Alabama history."

One of Miss Tutwiler's most conspicuous achievements as a social reformer was to obtain state support for the higher education and the vocational training of women. In seeking to accomplish these goals she was a tireless and vigorous campaigner. For several decades this "busy, white-haired woman with the face of a saint, clad in a faded black skirt, coat of obsolete fashion, and bonnet slipped sideways and backwards,"[1] endeavored to extend the educational opportunities for women in Alabama.

It was in 1880 that Julia Tutwiler seriously began her efforts to induce the Alabama legislature to provide adequate cultural and vocational education for women. This was the year she delivered her pioneer paper to the Alabama Educational Association on the merits of state-supported vocational instruction of women at the college level. Responsive to her urging, in 1889 the Alabama Educational Association adopted a resolution calling on the legislature to establish an industrial institute and college for the white women of the state.

Before this could be accomplished, Alabama Polytechnic Institute at Auburn, the state's land-grant institution, began to admit women, beginning with the session 1892-93. At this time Auburn was still functioning largely as a literary or classical college. After 1890 its facilities for the teaching of agriculture and engineering were steadily improved.[2]

What Julia Tutwiler wanted, however, was a state institution devoted solely to meeting the vocational needs of women. Finally, after a decade of effort to win popular and legislative support, she had the satisfaction in February, 1893, of seeing the legislature provide for the establishment of a "first-class industrial school for the education of white girls in the state of Alabama in industrial and scientific branches." In view of her ardent advocacy of the establishment of this school and her eminent position as an educator, it is not surprising that the new school's board of trustees in June, 1895, offered her the presidency of the school after considering eight candidates.[3]

Because of her deep interest in vocational education for women and her record as a progressive educator, one might have expected Julia Tutwiler to become president of this new women's vocational school. Apparently for some period of time she weighed the offer before she declined it. Very likely the determining factor in her decision was the refusal of the new school's board of trustees to accept the invitation of the Livingston Normal College to locate the industrial school in Livingston on land adjacent to the older institution. There had been considerable rivalry among various towns as to the site of the new school and the winner was the small town of Montevallo.

Whatever the reason for Miss Tutwiler's decision in the late summer of 1896 not to accept the Montevallo presidency, she devoted herself to another of her interests: the unqualified admission of women to the University of Alabama. This latter was a natural project for her to undertake. Her father had been a member of the University's first faculty and had been offered its presidency in 1868 and in 1874. She herself had lived in Tuscaloosa from 1876 to 1881 as a member of the faculty of the Tuscaloosa Female College. Many of her relatives and her professional colleagues were graduates or members of the University's faculty and administration. To her the University was the capstone of the state's system of public education. Women, therefore, should have the privilege of attendance.

To be sure, Julia Tutwiler was not alone in thinking that the state had an obligation to make higher education available to women.[4] For some decades after Reconstruction, however, the difficulties attendant upon the re-establishment of the University and the continuing conservative attitude with respect to the role of women militated against early adoption of the principle of co-education. With the appearance of a more progressive climate of opinion in the 1890's, Julia Tutwiler was encouraged to undertake a campaign to win acceptance of the principle. She set forth her arguments favoring co-education in a paper for the July, 1891, meeting of the Alabama Educational Association. She presented a comprehensive survey of Biblical and historical examples of women's free and equal association with men. She then expressed her belief that the ideal family should contain boys and girls so that each sex would grow up in companionship and in awareness of each other's strong and weak

qualities. Miss Tutwiler found fault with the civili-
zation of those peoples who, like the Mohammedans,
isolated their women and shut them off from participation in social activities. She then asked her
listeners to consider the odd aspects of the contemporary situation in Alabama. She pointed out that
in the usual social situations boys and girls freely
talked, walked and rode together. Why then, she
asked, was there any disapproval of allowing the
sexes to be together in the classroom? She concluded
by espousing the adoption of the principle of co-
education.[5]

In addition to such efforts to gain public and
organizational support for the idea of co-education,
Julia Tutwiler also sought to win the help of friends
and acquaintances. She wrote letters to various persons in public life, to presidents and members of
women's clubs, and to presidents of other educational institutions. Once while visiting in the home
of former Governor Thomas H. Watts, she induced
him, somewhat in fun, to outline a proposed legal
claim for damages against the state on behalf of
women deprived of their opportunities for higher
education.[6]

Finally, in midsummer of 1892, the board of
trustees of the University was willing to try a qualified form of co-education provided this was acceptable to the faculty. Preceding this decision, the
board had accorded to Miss Tutwiler the courtesy

and privilege of a hearing. She was at some pains to make it clear to the trustees of the University that "it was no joke to be robbing earnest and ambitious young women of opportunities to which they were justly entitled, and which they so much desired." The University faculty committee then studied the proposal and reported favorably early in 1893. So the decision stood to "admit young women of not less than 18 years of age, of good character, and antecedents, who are able to stand the necessary examinations" for entrance to the sophomore class or higher. A required proviso was that "suitable homes and protection" be provided. This first decision to prohibit the admission of women as freshmen very possibly was due to the ideas and influence of Miss Tutwiler herself. She believed that such a limitation had several desirable features. For example, of necessity the first women admitted to the University would be at least sophomores, hence already tried and mature students. Furthermore, the advanced standing requirement for the admission of women to the University would have the effect of lessening first-year competition for students and thus protect to some extent the women's colleges and normal schools.

In the autumn of 1893 the first two women students entered the University. For several years the number of women students was small, quite possibly because of the difficulty in finding living accommodations except, of course, for those whose homes were in Tuscaloosa. Yet the outstanding academic success of these first coeds clearly vindicated the confidence of Miss Tutwiler and others that women could meet the University's academic standards. And so in July, 1897, the University's board of trustees voted to remove the prohibition on the entrance of freshman women. Henceforth, effective with the autumn session of 1897, women were accepted and admitted to all rights and privileges of the University of Alabama.

However, Julia Tutwiler realized that her goal of opening to women the opportunity for higher education was not yet fully realized. Until the University provided housing for its women students, the victory for the principle of co-education seemed more apparent than it was real. At this juncture she was fortunate to secure a helpful ally in the new president of the University, James Knox Powers. Powers had previously been president of the Normal College at Florence. Together they had served as delegates from Alabama to the 1893 International Education Congress in Chicago. While talking with Powers at the University commencement exercises in 1898 she asked his assistance in finding a house where women students could live together co-operatively and inexpensively. At first Powers doubted that she could get enough women students from outside Tuscaloosa to fill such a co-operative house.

It was then agreed between them that the University
would provide a rent-free dwelling and that Miss
Tutwiler would assume the responsibility for some
of the furnishings and for recruiting ten women
students to live in it.[7]

Events moved rapidly in this final stage of Julia
Tutwiler's advocacy of higher education for the
women of Alabama. A two-story residence fronting
on University Avenue, near the home of the president of the University, was purchased with University funds and made ready for the opening of the
autumn 1898 session. In fitting tribute to the selfless spirit who had campaigned so long and so well
for the admission of women to the University it was
named the Julia S. Tutwiler Annex.

Meanwhile Miss Tutwiler bestirred herself to find
ten qualified young women whose parents were willing to allow them to attend the University as dormitory students. She overcame lingering conservative
ideas by reminding the parents that the male students at the University were none other than the
members of neighboring families. If these young
men were acceptable in homes, then they were
equally acceptable, she pointed out, as classmates at
the University. Success crowned her efforts and
when the University opened for the first semester
of the 1898-99 session ten women, all graduates of
her own normal school at Livingston, were enrolled
and in residence at the Julia S. Tutwiler Annex.

Miss Tutwiler visited the new University women's residence from time to time to see that the housing, financial, and academic arrangements were working out to the satisfaction of all. On different occasions she took with her groups of her own Livingston students who were planning to enroll the next year at the University. She took these visitors to see the co-operative dormitory and to hear lectures and visit laboratories in an early example of what we think of as sub-freshman orientation.[8]

In 1907 at the celebration of its seventy-fifth anniversary, the University of Alabama awarded Julia Tutwiler an honorary doctorate of law. This was a fitting recognition of her many outstanding contributions to the advancement of public education in Alabama. Although she had never attended an institution of higher learning in Alabama and had never received an academic degree, she had made numerous contributions in the field of education. In particular she had worked for the development of teacher training, vocational education, and the admission of women to the state university. Further recognition by the University of Alabama of Miss Tutwiler's interest in the university education of the women of the state came in 1915 when the first large women's dormitory erected on the campus was named Julia Tutwiler Hall in her honor.

Although Julia Tutwiler's concern with the improvement and extension of education was deep and

continuing, it by no means absorbed all of her reforming energy. She was sensitive to people's needs
and was imbued with an awareness of the responsibilities implicit in Christian discipleship. Religious
by family training and personal conviction, she possessed the qualities of charity and love. Thus it was
that her sincere regard for the welfare of others was
manifested in quick sympathy and help for those
who were "distressed, poor, ignorant, erring, wayward or suffering."

Many of Julia Tutwiler's greatest contributions
lay in the realm of her humanitarian and charitable
activities, especially in the field of prison reform.
Throughout the United States in the latter part of
the nineteenth century there remained much to be
done if prisons were to perform a useful and humane
function. In far too many instances prisoners were
herded together with little or no effort to separate
young from old and first offenders from hardened
criminals. It was customary to think of imprison-
ment solely as a punishment meted out by society.
Furthermore, in most cases prison authorities and
attendants were appointed through political influence and had little, if any, training or special qualifications for the work. Since most of the prison staff
thus held office by political favoritism it is understandable that they disliked outside reformers.

One of the unfortunate aftermaths of the emanci-
pation of the Negroes had been an increase in crimes

and misdemeanors. After 1865 the prison system in
the southern states was inadequate to meet the
problem. There were not enough southern prisons,
or funds to construct sufficient new ones, to house
all of the offenders, most of whom were Negroes.
Largely out of expediency the southern states
adopted the practice of leasing, or farming out, their
convicts to private persons or companies. These
private individuals or companies assumed the cus-
todial care in return for the use of the labor of the
prisoners and a small payment to the state. Quite
naturally, this convict lease system proved to be a
moneymaker both to the state, which received a
rental charge from the lessee for each convict, and
to the lessee who had the unlimited time and labor
of the convicts. It was inevitable that this practice
of hiring out prisoners to private persons should
lead to serious abuses. Both the state and the private lessee stood to gain money through the enforced labor of the convict and neither was required
to assume responsibility for his welfare. At a time
when the South was poverty-stricken, reluctant to
give status to the Negro, and still convinced that
the primary purpose of incarceration was to punish
the convict for his misdeeds, the adoption of this
convict lease system is understandable. Yet it was
brutal, degrading, and totally lacking in elements
of the older southern tradition of paternalism or of
the newer humanitarianism.

In a somewhat accidental way in the winter of
1879-80 the attention of Miss Tutwiler was drawn
to the need for prison reform. She was then teaching and living in Tuscaloosa. A servant girl had
been arrested and jailed and Julia Tutwiler went to
offer assistance. At the town jail she was shocked
by the apparent lack of interest in the moral and
spiritual welfare of the inmates and by the inade-
quacies and unhealthful conditions. Ever quick and
humane in her response to the needs of others, Julia
Tutwiler at once embarked upon a personal and
charitable program of visits and assistance to individual prisoners in jails and prisons. To meet the
immediate situation in the Tuscaloosa jail she induced some other strong-minded friends to go with
her to visit the prisoners, to read the Bible to them,
and to advise and counsel them. She secured donations of Bibles from publishing houses for distribution to the jail inmates.

Even in the midst of her first efforts to bring the
spirit of Christian love and charity to the inmates
of the Tuscaloosa jail, Miss Tutwiler recognized
the need for a comprehensive attack on the problem. To be sure, much of her inspiration came from
her naturally deep and charitable interest in the
spiritual redemption of others. But she was quick
to recognize the obligation on society to provide
corrective and educational programs for the betterment of the inmates of jails and prisons. Further-

more she remembered the fine work she had seen carried on in Germany by the Institute of Deaconesses at Kaiserswerth. This organization had pioneered in extensive religious, charitable, and educational work among criminals. It had also established a reformatory school where women inmates had been treated more like penitents than prisoners. Hence it is understandable that she organized the Tuscaloosa Benevolent Association and embarked on a program to win popular interest in prison reform. The first project of the new association was to distribute a fact-finding questionnaire late in 1880 to the jailers in each county of the state.

When the replies to the questionnaire on conditions in the county jails were tabulated it appeared that only a few of the jails were suitably provided with fresh water, sewerage facilities, or furnaces to provide heat in the winter. Nor was much interest reported in the personal welfare of the prisoners. Widespread public interest was aroused by the publication of this information in the newspapers. As a result of her initiative and her advocacy of the need for improvement, Julia Tutwiler quickly became known as a champion of prison reform. Nor did she have to wait long for the first results of her humanitarian interest in the welfare of prisoners. In December, 1880, the Alabama legislature adopted a bill to improve the physical conditions in the county jails. The new act made it a specific duty

of the sheriffs to see that county jails were supplied
with wholesome water, toilet facilities, and with
heat in cold weather. The credit went to Julia Tutwiler for arousing the public sentiment which pro-
duced this measure.[9]

When she moved to Livingston in July of 1881
Miss Tutwiler transferred her personal activity on
behalf of prisoners to the local jail. She was convinced of the need to provide prisoners with a
program of religious instruction if they were ever
to be taught to shun their former errors. Regularly
on Sundays she conducted religious services in the
Livingston jail. She often took with her a group of
volunteer assistants from the student body of the
Livingston Normal College. These jail services
usually included the singing of hymns, the recitation of Biblical selections and prayers, and an
informal sermon by Miss Tutwiler. In her talks she
placed particular emphasis on the interest of Jesus
in a repentant sinner and the strength of His par-
doning grace. Many of the prisoners, who were
mostly Negro men, were led to ask for her prayers.
Bibles were given to those who had memorized the
greatest number of Biblical verses during the week.[10]

Once Julia Tutwiler's attention had been drawn
to the needs of persons imprisoned in local jails, it
was inevitable that she would also acquaint herself
with conditions in the state prisons as well. Sometime in the mid-1880's she made her first visit to

the convict camps in the iron mines near Birmingham. It was an impression she never forgot. She was distressed by the dull, hopeless misery in the eyes of the convicts, who neither asked for nor expected alleviation of their hard lot as miners and convicts. This experience led her to expand her role as an "angel of the stockades" or jails to include prison camps as well. She made it a regular practice to board a train late in the evening at Livingston and travel through the night to Birmingham. During the next day she went to the prison camps located in the coal mines outside the city. She distributed books, papers, magazines and pictures among white and Negro prisoners. She provided school books, slates and pencils purchased from funds contributed by interested friends. One of her larger projects was the establishment of small libraries for the use of prisoners.[11]

With this extension of her concern for the welfare of prisoners to include state prison camps as well as local jails, Julia Tutwiler greatly broadened the scope of her reforming zeal. It was fortunate that she now had the devoted and continuing support of at least one influential organization. It was in 1882 or 1883 that the local units in Alabama of the Woman's Christian Temperance Union invited Miss Tutwiler to join the organization and serve as state chairman of prison and jail work. She at once accepted this appointment as "prison superintendent."

At the 1885 and 1886 annual meetings she reported in some detail on her work and on her recommendations for reform. She was convinced that no very substantial improvement in prison conditions could be accomplished until the convict lease system itself was abolished. But she was realistic enough to recognize that the convict lease system was too profitable to the state treasury and to private employers for it to be abolished easily and quickly. This was in spite of the fact that she believed the system had the effect of placing the state in the role of providing a training school for the education of criminals.[12]

Miss Tutwiler despaired in the mid-eighties of winning the necessary political support for the abolition of convict leasing. If she could not accomplish such a comprehensive change in the state's penal procedures she could, she believed, work for the gradual acceptance of minor but important reforms. During her long years of prison reform activity, she learned how to accept stoically much criticism and many discouragements. There was adverse comment concerning her habit of traveling about the state at odd hours in order to visit prisons and convict camps or to press her views upon legislators at the state capital. She often observed to sympathetic friends her belief that "God and one make a majority" in such matters. She learned to take courage from the thought that "this life of mortal breath is but a suburb of the life elysian."

Such singleness of devotion to welfare work among the prisoners slowly brought results. By a series of acts in 1883, 1885, and 1886 the legislature gave authority to the governor and a prison board to define rules for the treatment of prisoners and to require convict labor lessees, under penalty of termination of their contracts, to live up to these minimum working and living standards. It was Julia Tutwiler's hope in 1887 to induce the state legislature to provide for the separation of criminals according to age, seriousness of offense, and previous penal record. Specifically, she advocated the construction by the state of a reformatory for the incarceration of young male prisoners. During her visits to the convict mining camps Miss Tutwiler had been particularly dismayed to see how many of the prisoners were young boys under sixteen years of age. In her effort to secure the passage of this measure establishing a boys' reformatory she prevailed upon her friends, colleagues, and various benevolent organizations to use their influence with individual legislators. To no avail. The legislators were indifferent to the need of separating youthful offenders from older and more habitual violators of the law and reluctant to spend state money to house prisoners.

In order to salvage something from this doomed effort to establish a reformatory, in the closing days of the 1887 session Miss Tutwiler hastened to Mont-

gomery from Livingston. If it was impossible to get
the whole loaf, she would settle for part. She proposed to one of her friends in the legislature that
an effort be made to secure the establishment by the
state of nighttime prison schools in the convict
camps. This proposal was agreeable to the legislators
and an act was passed for the organization of prison
schools. The penurious attitude of the legislature
was reflected, however, in the scanty financial support provided. Nevertheless an important precedent
had been set. And to Miss Tutwiler and to Alabama go the credit for the establishment in 1887
of the first prison school of any importance in the
South.[13] It well may be that this was the reform
measure about which a popular story concerning
Julia Tutwiler was circulated. It was said that at
the moment when a prominent legislator was about
to vote against her bill, he chanced to look up in the
gallery. There he saw Miss Tutwiler in the posture
of prayer. This so impressed him that he changed
his mind, voted for the proposal and it carried.[14]

The effort that Miss Tutwiler had put forth to
secure the enactment of this legislation authorizing
the establishment of prison schools was more than
matched by her energy and ingenuity in implemen-
tation. She was disappointed but not disheartened
by the fact that the act did not provide funds for
the construction of any classrooms. She now busied
herself with the actual arrangements for the open-

ing of a school for convict miners at the Pratt Mines, outside Birmingham. In May of 1887 she went herself to the vice-president of the Tennessee Coal, Iron, and Railroad Company, lessee of these convicts, and asked him for help. She convinced this man of business that the provision of educational facilities would have a beneficial effect on the prisoners and also make them better workers. The company agreed to make available a room in which the classes could be held. Next it was necessary to find an interested and capable person to do the actual teaching of the fundamentals of reading and writing and the essentials of religious principles to ignorant criminals. Miss Tutwiler believed that the prejudice against special treatment for convicts was too strong in Alabama to make it possible to find a suitable candidate there. After several weeks of search in Chicago she employed a young man who was particularly interested in this type of endeavor.[15]

Finally, late in August, 1887, as a direct result of Julia Tutwiler's optimism and perseverance the first prison school in Alabama was opened at the Pratt Mines. Present for the inaugural services, at her specific invitation, was the Governor, Thomas Seay. When the bill had been under consideration and there were doubts as to what possible good effect a prison school could have, she had told him of her confidence in the measure. She realized that the establishment of these schools in the convict camps was but a small step in the right direction. Small step though it was, she had assured him that there was great value in having even one "auger-hole in the roof of the darkest cavern in hell, and let in one ray of heavenly light." Thus was inaugurated one of her most practical prison reforms.[16]

In the meantime Miss Tutwiler continued her practice of visiting jails and prison camps in order to bring a personal message of hope to the inmates. Eventually the night train journeys of over a hundred miles between Livingston and the prison camps in the mines took their toll of her health. Two long spells of bronchitis brought on by the hardships of these visits forced her reluctantly after 1891 to curtail somewhat these lengthy trips. She continued to make her regular reports as the prison superintendent of the Alabama W. C. T. U. Also, she was tireless in the use of her voice and pen in pointing out weaknesses in prison administration and additional reforms that needed to be made.

As the representative of Alabama at the International Historical Congress of Charities and Corrections meeting in Chicago in 1893, Julia Tutwiler reported on the major developments in the field of social work and reform in Alabama for the past twenty years. She praised the work done for the insane and described the progress in the handling of prison inmates. Then she set forth a frank criticism of the state for failing to provide adequately for other unfortunates such as Negro orphans, the feebleminded, and those physically ill.[17]

In the field of penal reform, progress was made slowly but surely. In 1895 the state expanded the program of prison schools by opening one at the Wetumpka Prison and requiring the attendance of white and Negro boys. In spite of Miss Tutwiler's continuing advocacy, no provision was made at this time for prison schools for women inmates. Her earlier efforts to interest individuals and organizations in penal reform now bore increasing fruit. Through the particular efforts of Mrs. R. D. Johnston of Birmingham, a co-worker in W. C. T. U. prison visiting work, the state finally established a reformatory school for white boys, the Alabama Boys' Industrial School, located at East Lake. Subsequently in 1911 the State of Alabama took a further step in providing for the rehabilitation of delinquents by establishing the Reform and Industrial School for Negro Boys at Mount Meigs. In the same year, a school for the training of wayward white girls was also founded.

In view of Julia Tutwiler's long-continuing interest in prison reform it was natural for her to participate in national organizations dedicated to social reform. From available partial records, it appears that she was active in the annual meetings of the National Charities Association. For a number of years she served as a delegate for the State of Ala-

bama to the International Society of Charities and
Corrections. Apparently it was customary for her to
attend at her own expense but to have the honor of
being the official state representative.[18]

After her retirement from the presidency of the
Livingston Normal College in 1910, Julia Tutwiler
used her additional leisure to carry on her activities
on behalf of prisoners. She was interested in 1911,
for example, in securing donations of cloth scraps
to be made into quilts by women inmates at the
state prison farm at Speigner. In a newspaper interview, she appealed for contributions to purchase an
organ for this penal institution. At another time,
she reiterated her hope that Alabama would finally
see fit to abolish the convict lease system. She also
advocated better supervision of the health of convicts
so as to detect and separate those with tuberculosis,
the provision of remunerative employment for men
in county jails, and the distribution of Bibles with
large print. The continuing practicality and com-
prehensiveness of her recommendations compels admiration and respect for this doughty old lady.[19]

Most of Miss Tutwiler's fame as a reformer rests
on her prison work, but there were at least two
other fields of endeavor in which she also gave
notable service: prohibition and the abolition of
war. Both of these interests grew naturally out of
her religious convictions. She stated, in 1906, that
she was "a member of quite a number of Associa-

tions which are working for the 'coming of the Kingdom': the International Peace Association, the Charities and Corrections Conference, the Prison Reform Association, the W. C. T. U., the Y. W. C. A., the Salvation Army, the Anti-Saloon League, ALL the different churches of this little town [of Livingston]."[20]

As a member of the W. C. T. U. she wrote this song:

PROHIBITION RALLY SONG

Where's the man who fears opinion?
He is not the friend for me.
Let him cringe to rum's dominion,
Sister, you and I are free.
So, let the cowards vote as they will,
I'm for prohibition still.
Prohibition, Prohibition,
I'm for prohibition still.[21]

Soon after she arrived in Livingston in 1881 Miss Tutwiler decided that saloons had no place in a small southern town with a girls' school. Forthwith she organized the townspeople and the students in a campaign to rid the town and the county of alcohol. It was a lively contest but soon both Livingston and the neighboring town of Sumterville were dry. There is a paucity of contemporary newspaper reference concerning Julia Tutwiler's prohibition campaign in Sumter County during the 1880's, but Sumter County, including the town of

Livingston, was made dry by an act of the state legislature approved on December 9, 1886. This act provided that on and after January 1, 1887, ". . . it shall be unlawful to sell, give away, or otherwise dispose of any spirituous, vinous or malt liquors, or alcoholic bitters, cordials or beverages of any kind in Sumter County." During the last two decades of the nineteenth century the Alabama General Assembly was especially friendly toward petitions from rural areas for the prohibition of liquor sales. No less than 467 churches, 78 schools, 37 towns, and 30 counties received such protection in the period from 1880 to 1899.[22]

The extent of Miss Tutwiler's activity in the international peace movement cannot be measured by available records. However, she wrote a poem for the International Peace Association to be sung at gatherings of this group. The first and last stanzas of her peace song are as follows:

THE STAR-SPANGLED BANNER OF PEACE

O, the world is aweary of battle and strife;
She is weary of death; she is longing for life;
And here, in her glory, Columbia stands,
A light round her brow, and a lamp in her hands,
She will guide, she will lead, and illumine the way,
'Till the nations of earth are all brothers for aye,
While her star-spangled banner shall peacefully wave
O'er the land of the free and the home of the brave.

    .   .   .   .

Let our banner be Thine, Prince of Peace and of Love;

On its staff for the eagle Thy baptismal dove;
Let the stars in its folds but betoken the one
That once led the wise men to the cradle, Thy throne,
And the stripes of bright crimson declare Thou hast bled
That man's blood nevermore by man's hand shall be shed;
Then the star-spangled banner in triumph shall wave,
O'er a nation—Thy freemen—for righteousness brave![23]

In this account of Miss Tutwiler's endeavors as a reformer and humanitarian there remains only the need to point out the nature and extent of her private charity. These details can best be supplied by making use of a letter she wrote in 1906, when she was inquiring into the possibility of securing a Carnegie teacher's pension. Her own income after retirement would be sufficient for her personal needs, she stated. The reason why she wished to secure a Carnegie pension of $2,000 a year was, she explained, to enable her to continue the "dearest pleasure" of life which was "liberality to others." She went on:

. . . I have my little personal charities: I employ a good religious colored woman to teach the Bible and sewing to the girls of the public school for the colored here; and a young man to teach the boys shoe mending. I am the *only* visitor to the jail and poorhouse. I teach in the former every Sunday afternoon, and generally carry some little gift to the inmates especially at Christmas and Thanksgiving. I have just fitted up a little chapel for the poorhouse with some help from the owners of the lumber mill. I am meeting all the expenses of a student in the Bible School in New York.[24]

This record of private benevolence when added to her public humanitarian and reform activities only serves to underline Julia Tutwiler's devotion to the welfare of mankind. Her unselfish devotion to the unfortunate, the ignorant, the poor and the needy mark her out as an ardent spirit filled with Christian charity.

5. Journey's End

JULIA TUTWILER suffered intermittent spells of illness in the six years between her retirement in June of 1910 and death in March of 1916. In the autumn of 1910, for example, she was "crippled up" and said to be suffering from sciatica. She apparently believed in the merits of fasting as a relief from such difficulties. In these last years of her life she remained fairly active and made many trips and visits. Nor did her good humor fail her. The Alabama Department of Archives had requested a picture. In sending it she wrote that her likeness might encourage young people to realize that homeliness need not prevent them from leading useful and happy lives.[1]

In August, 1915, the Birmingham Writer's Club unanimously elected Miss Tutwiler to honorary membership. This was in recognition of her national prominence gained by her writings and by her efforts to elevate mankind. Surely this recognition must have pleased her, particularly as she was then living in Birmingham. At about this time one of her nieces asked her to get her writings together. Miss Tutwiler's good-humored reply was, "No, moderately good poetry is like moderately good eggs, nobody wants it."[2]

When the first large dormitory for women was erected in 1914 on the campus of the University of Alabama it was decided to name it in her honor. Just before Miss Tutwiler died she received a friendly letter from the residents of the dormitory expressing their pleasure in having her name on the building.[3]

After a lingering illness Julia Tutwiler died of cancer in Birmingham on March 24, 1916, approximately a month short of her seventy-fifth birthday. In accordance with her expressed wishes her body was cremated, although this was somewhat unusual in Alabama at that time. Her reason for specifying cremation was her belief that this process would help lessen the spread of disease.[4]

At the graveside rites in accordance with Miss Tutwiler's request, the Episcopal burial service was read by a minister of the Presbyterian Church, the church of which she had long been a member. No doubt she requested this particular form of burial service because of her longstanding liking for the liturgy of the Episcopal Church. Among the many floral offerings at the grave were those of the women students of the University of Alabama; the students and alumnae of the Alabama Normal School; the citizens of Livingston; the chapters of the Daughters of the American Revolution in Livingston and Tuscaloosa; the chapters of the United Daughters of the Confederacy in Livingston and Tuscaloosa; and the W. C. T. U. branch in Tuscaloosa.[5]

Memorial services for Julia Tutwiler were held in Birmingham, Tuscaloosa and Livingston. The service in Livingston was held under the auspices of the mayor and town council. It included vespers, a eulogy, and many of Julia Tutwiler's favorite hymns. The newspaper account concluded:

As has been said, the audience was most appreciative. The whole student body of 250 or more girls, College faculty, the town authorities, the ministers of the different denominations, the women who owe much to her in their intellectual lives, the children who have received many a smile and kindly word, the men who toiled side by side with her for a common aim—the well-being of womankind—all were here to bear testimony by their presence to the fact of the passing of a great woman.[6]

Thus it was that at her death, Julia Tutwiler received widespread acclaim for her contributions to the welfare of Alabama and for her noble and

inspiring character. The nature of her educational
and humanitarian activities was fully set forth. Her
personal qualities of sympathy, energy, creativeness,
and self-sacrifice were praised. One of these edi-
torial tributes said of her:

Always on the watch to help aspiring humanity with
her means as well as her mind, she was equally ready to
reach out her hand to the hopeless. . . .

Whenever she set out to accomplish anything, she gave
herself wholeheartedly to the cause, never counting the
cost to herself. . . .

The name of Miss Julia Tutwiler has been a household
word in Alabama for a generation. And it is safe to say
that so long as lofty ideals and noble achievement are
honored, her name will live secure among those of other
great spirits of her own state and of the South.[7]

Soon after Julia Tutwiler's death, the Alabama
W. C. T. U. honored her. A permanent collection
of books on the topic of temperance was placed in
each institution of higher learning and in each
prison as a memorial to her temperance and prison
activities. In their announcement, the executive
committee declared this action to be

In view of the fact that the Woman's Christian Temperance Union was the first organization under which
Miss Julia S. Tutwiler worked, and that her great work
in this state for prison reform was done as State Superintendent of the Prison Reform Department of the Alabama
W. C. T. U. for over 32 years; and in recognition also of
her deep interest in the education of the young people of
this state. . . .[8]

In her will, Julia Tutwiler directed that all of her property in Livingston was to be converted into a scholarship loan fund for the "Girls of Alabama." By 1926, the sum available for such loans amounted to $15,000 and it was reported that a total of 125 students had been assisted. In death, therefore, Julia Tutwiler continued to give financial support to the girls of Alabama in their quest for education and training.[9]

In the years following her death, the friends of Julia Tutwiler sought to keep her name and the record of her accomplishments before the people of Alabama. In April, 1917, during the meetings of the Alabama Educational Association, a group of Miss Tutwiler's former pupils and friends arranged for special memorial services in her honor. At this time, a life-sized portrait was presented to the State of Alabama to be hung in the state archives building.[10]

In 1923, the admirers of Julia Tutwiler were active in two projects designed to accord her a larger measure of public recognition. Unfortunately, neither was successful. One was an effort to induce the state legislature to select her for the second, and final, place allotted to the State of Alabama in the nation's Hall of Fame. The other proposal, also unsuccessful, was to change the name of the Alabama Normal College at Livingston to the Julia S. Tutwiler State Normal School.[11]

In May of 1926, the graduates of the Livingston Normal College began a drive for a fund to honor Julia Tutwiler. It was hoped that sufficient money would be collected to build a new school auditorium. Three years later, in August, 1929, the State Board of Education, at the suggestion of the Livingston Alumni Association and with the recommendation of President G. W. Brock, renamed the administration and classroom building the Julia Tutwiler Hall. At that time, the Alumni Association had collected about $5,000 and this sum was to be spent in renovating the building and placing in it a memorial tablet to Julia Tutwiler.[12]

In 1930, a highway bridge on state route 39, across the Tombigbee River, at Gainesville, was named the Julia S. Tutwiler Bridge. This bridge is located a few miles north of Livingston.[13]

During the observance of the centennial of the University of Alabama, a portrait of Julia Tutwiler was presented in May, 1931, to the University. Through the efforts of the Alabama Federation of Women's Clubs, funds had been collected for the purpose. The painting was the work of Bradley Walker Tomlin and showed Julia Tutwiler at the time she was a student at Vassar College in 1866-67. The portrait was declared to be a "splendid representation of a beautiful subject" and to be particularly appropriate in that it suggested "the things Miss Tutwiler valued." With elaborate dedicatory ceremony, the portrait was hung in Doster Hall, the center of social life for the women of the University.[14]

Subsequently, a memorial tablet to Julia Tutwiler, the work of Geneva Mercer, one of her former students, was placed in the rotunda of the Alabama state capitol in 1933. In addition to a marble bust of Miss Tutwiler, a verse from her own poem "Alabama," and a quotation from the Bible, this tribute contains the following inscription:

Julia Strudwick Tutwiler, teacher, poet, prison reformer, patriot, lover of humanity, beauty and truth. Pioneer for industrial and University education for women in Alabama.

In 1937, at the first Alabama Normal College commencement after Dr. G. W. Brock's retirement in September, 1936, the alumni presented a portrait of Julia Tutwiler to the college. Her long and distinguished educational career was cited, as well as her "loving kindness" and "the wonderful capacity she had of imparting knowledge."[15]

A dormitory on the campus of Alabama College has been named for Julia Tutwiler, to commemorate particularly her part in the creation of that institution. Similarly, the Julia Tutwiler Prison for women, located about one mile north of Wetumpka, perpetuates the memory of her notable efforts to abolish the convict lease system and to improve prison conditions.

Finally, there needs to be recorded Julia Tutwiler's selection in October, 1953, as one of the first eleven persons named to the Alabama Hall of Fame.[16] The plaques for these honored persons are in the State Archives and History Building.

Hers reads:

JULIA STRUDWICK TUTWILER

1841-1916

Educator

She opened doors of higher learning to women at the University and in schools for teachers. She brought light into prisons and led the way to far-reaching social reforms.

Notes

1. DAUGHTER OF THE SOUTH

1. Much of the biographical information about Henry Tutwiler comes from clippings, memoranda, and pamphlets to be found in the Tutwiler Collection in the Library of the University of Alabama. All statements of fact concerning Julia Tutwiler's life and quotations not otherwise credited are based on materials in this same collection. Hereafter cited as Tutwiler Collection (University).

2. There is some evidence to suggest that this may have been the Alabama Institute of Literature and Natural Philosophy, a manual labor school established by the Alabama Baptist Convention in 1833. This early college was representative of several attempts, especially before 1860 in the South, to combine self-help and academic studies. Teachers were expected to share with the students in the performance of manual work. If Tutwiler did teach here it well may be that later family discussions about the experience served to familiarize Julia with this early type of vocational training.

3. Tutwiler prepared in 1877 a short *Sketch of Greene Springs School for Thirty Years.* Late in her life Julia Tutwiler wrote a draft "Memoranda for Biographical Sketch of Henry Tutwiler." A pamphlet published by the Hale County Historical Society at Havana, Alabama, in 1947, contains an address given on May 1, 1947, by Walter B. Jones on "The Greene Springs School." Very little if any source material survived the various fires that afflicted the school.

4. Much of this information about Julia Tutwiler's childhood comes from a letter of Katherine Tutwiler Meriwether to Netta Tut-

wiler McCorvey, undated but written after Miss Tutwiler's death. Tutwiler Collection (University).

5. See Minnie Clare Boyd, *Alabama in the Fifties: A Social Study* (New York: Columbia University Press, 1931), p. 128, for details on teachers' salaries. Information about landholding and slaveholding in Greene County on the eve of the War will be found in Frank Lawrence Owsley, *Plain Folk of the Old South* (Baton Rouge: Louisiana State University Press, 1949), pp. 77, 84-85, 181-188.

6. An examination of the *Philadelphia Directory* for the years from 1854 to 1861 indicates that the location of this French and English School was frequently changed. In 1859 the school was located at 1530 Spruce Street. It would appear that this particular school was selected by the family on the recommendation of one of Tutwiler's University of Virginia classmates who resided in Philadelphia.

7. Sometime after 1865 Tutwiler gave an "Address to the Freedmen of Alabama" in which he stated that he had formerly owned more than twenty slaves but had never bought one except at the request of the slave and had never sold one. He declared that he had endeavored to treat his slaves as he would have had them treat him. He expressed the belief that his former slaves would divide their last crumbs with his family should the Tutwilers come to want. Undated, incomplete MS in the possession of G. Burke Johnston of Blacksburg, Virginia.

8. This poem is included in the printed and unprinted materials collected by Dean Eoline Wallace Moore of Birmingham-Southern College and deposited in the Tutwiler Collection (University).

2. RESTLESS SEARCHER

1. Tutwiler family tradition and an article in the *Livingston* [Ala.] *Journal* for July 18, 1885, state that Julia Tutwiler gave instruction in French and German during the half year she was at Vassar College. However there is no official record extant that lists her as a teacher on the faculty for this first academic year of 1865-66.

2. In 1867 the Alabama legislature took part of Greene County to form Hale County, named in honor of a Confederate army hero.

3. Most of this information concerning the tenure of Julia Tutwiler at the Greensboro Academy was gained from a batch of clippings from the *Alabama Beacon* in the Tutwiler Collection (University)

and from two letters of former students quoted in Clara L. Pitts, "Julia Strudwick Tutwiler" (unpublished Ed.D. dissertation, George Washington University, 1942), pp. 63-66. Hereafter cited as Pitts, "Tutwiler."

4. This version has been adapted from the draft included in her short paper on Maury prepared while she was at Livingston Normal College.

5. There are only scattered and fragmentary source materials available concerning the details of this European tour. The Laird incident is related in her paper on Maury. It also figures in her undated MS, "A London Episode."

6. The information about Miss Thomas comes from the biography by Edith Finch, *Carey Thomas of Bryn Mawr* (New York: Harper & Bros., 1947).

7. The presentation that follows in this chapter is based almost entirely on six letters and an address. The six letters were written between August 21, 1873, and March 29, 1875, and are apparently the only ones to survive. On July 16, 1891, at the annual meeting of the National Educational Association, she gave a paper on "A Year in a German Model School." This is to be found in the *Journal of Proceedings and Addresses of the National Educational Association, 1891.* Hereafter cited as *NEA Journal, 1891.*

8. *NEA Journal, 1891,* p. 167.

9. *Ibid.,* pp. 164-167.

10. *Ibid.,* pp. 168-169.

11. Much of this information concerning her authorship of this poem comes from personal interviews and correspondence by Anne Gary Pannell with Miss Tutwiler's surviving relatives and friends.

12. Julia Tutwiler to Netta Tutwiler, n.p., December 3, 1874, and March 27, 1875. Tutwiler Collection (University).

13. Julia Tutwiler to Netta Tutwiler, n.p., March 27 and March 29, 1875. Tutwiler Collection (University).

3. CONSTRUCTIVE PIONEER

1. Richard G. Boone, *Education in the United States: Its History from the Earliest Settlements* (New York: D. Appleton and Co., 1893), pp. 380-381. Women were not admitted to full membership in the National Teachers Association until 1866. Willard S. Elsbree,

The American Teacher: Evolution of a Profession in a Democracy (New York: American Book Co., 1939), p. 265.

2. Quoted in Pitts, "Tutwiler," p. 72.

3. "The Charities of Paris: What One Woman Can Do" will be found in *The Churchman*, XXXIX (1879), pp. 240-241. "The Technical Education of Women" will be found in the *National Journal of Education*, III (November, 1882), pp. 201-207.

4. Milton Lee Orr, *State Supported Colleges for Women* (Nashville: George Peabody College for Teachers, 1930), pp. 131-132.

5. Carlos G. Smith and Henry Tutwiler had married sisters, hence Julia was his niece.

6. Printed notice in the possession of G. W. Brock, Livingston, Alabama.

7. Oscar W. Hyatt, *The Development of Secondary Education in Alabama Prior to 1920* (Nashville: George Peabody College for Teachers, 1933), pp. 71-74.

8. Address given by Frank Grove on "Julia Tutwiler, the Educator," on May 11, 1939. Tutwiler Collection (University).

9. Rev. B[enjamin] F[ranklin] Riley, *Alabama As It Is: or, The Immigrant's and Capitalist's Guide Book to Alabama* (Montgomery: W. C. Holt, Published for the State, 1887), pp. 103-104.

10. National Educational Association, *Journal of Proceedings and Addresses: 1884* (Boston: National Educational Association, 1885), pp. 16, 26. In 1870 the earlier National Teachers Association had become the National Educational Association. Subsequently in 1906 the name was changed to the National Education Association of the United States. There was considerable variation in the size of membership and amount of influence of this organization between 1870 and 1900. The membership did not reach 15,000 in this period and fell to 625 in 1885. However, most of the influential educators of the period were active in its conventions.

11. National Educational Association, *Journal of Proceedings and Addresses: 1886* (Salem: National Educational Association, 1887), pp. 26, 262-263, 266.

12. National Educational Association, *Journal of Proceedings and Addresses: 1890* (Topeka: National Educational Association, 1890), p. 601. The contents of this paper on "Our Brother in Stripes, in the School-Room" will be discussed in a subsequent chapter.

13. National Educational Association, *Journal of Proceedings and Addresses: 1891* (New York: National Educational Association, 1891), pp. 161-169, 571.

14. National Educational Association, *Journal of Proceedings and Addresses: 1892* (New York: National Educational Association, 1893), pp. 309-310.

15. *Proceedings of the International Congress of Education of the World's Columbian Exposition: Chicago, July 25-28, 1893* (New York: National Educational Association, 1895), p. 385. The other two Alabama representatives were James K. Powers, President of the Florence State Normal College; and Professor E. R. Eldridge of the Troy State Normal School.

The World's Congress of Representative Women was held in Chicago May 15-22, 1893, under the auspices of the Woman's Branch of the World's Congress Auxiliary. It was said to be "the largest and most representative gathering of women ever convened in this or any other country." May Wright Sewall, ed. *The World's Congress of Representative Women* . . . (Chicago: Rand, McNally & Co., 1894), pp. v, 5-6. Miss Tutwiler's name is not listed as one of the major participants.

See Chapter 4 for details on Miss Tutwiler's paper on humanitarian and charitable developments of that era in Alabama.

16. "Is Self Support Possible for Girls During the Years of Secondary Education?" Abstract of a paper read by Julia Tutwiler in the Women's Building of the Columbian Fair, Chicago, reprinted from the *Daily Register,* n.p., n.d. Tutwiler Collection (University).

17. It would appear that Julia Tutwiler made an extensive tour of Europe in the summer of 1886. See clipping from the *Christian Observer,* dated August 11, 1886, in which "A Lady Traveling in Europe" recounted features of her visit to Trieste, the Adriatic Gulf, Corfu, and Athens. Tutwiler Collection (University).

18. The original Chautauqua Assembly was held in 1874 at Fair Point on Lake Chautauqua, in western New York. One of the two founders was John Heyl Vincent, later a Bishop in the Methodist Church. From his birth in 1832 until 1837, young Vincent resided in Tuscaloosa, Alabama, and was one of the Sunday school pupils of Henry Tutwiler.

19. *Montgomery Advertiser,* June 15, 1885. *Livingston Journal,* September 26, 1895. Interview with Miss Nicholene Bishop by Anne Gary Pannell. Tutwiler Collection (University).

20. Julia Tutwiler was one of the 1,470 eminent American women listed in Frances E. Willard and Mary A. Livermore, *A Woman of the Century* . . .; *Biographical Sketches* . . . *of Leading Women in All Walks of Life* (Buffalo: Charles Wells Moulton, 1893), p. 728.

21. Due to the generosity of a friend, Frank R. Chambers, Julia Tutwiler had money for this purpose. In 1910 the remaining funds, in excess of $6,000, were placed in a Julia S. Tutwiler Scholarship Loan Fund devoted to "the assistance of needy Alabama girls in obtaining an education." Typescript of trust declaration furnished by Mrs. T. C. McCorvey.

22. Inez H. Weed, "Julia S. Tutwiler," *American Magazine*, September, 1910. Typewritten copy furnished by Mrs. T. C. McCorvey.

23. Julia S. Tutwiler, "How the Girls of Alabama Pushed Open the Doors of the State University; Some Ancient History," n.p., n.d. Tutwiler Collection (University).

24. Report by Julia S. Tutwiler, found in *Minutes of the Alabama W. C. T. U.*, 1895, cited in Pitts, "Tutwiler," p. 211. Miss Tutwiler told the members of the W. C. T. U. that she had lost "uninsured pianos and furniture" belonging to her. *Livingston Journal*, June 13, 1895.

25. *Our Southern Home* (Livingston), September 22, 1898, cited in Pitts, "Tutwiler," p. 111. Letter from Wade Hampton Coleman, Jr., November 17, 1955.

26. Elise Cooke Ward, "A Tribute To a Great Alabamian" [newspaper clipping], n.p., n.d. Frank Grove's tribute in the *Alabama School Journal*, September, 1931. Mildred Sandison Fenner and Jean Conder Soule, "Julia Tutwiler, Southern Pioneer," *National Education Association Journal* (November, 1946), pp. 498-499.

27. "A Letter to the Members of the New Legislature from their Mother Alabama" [broadside], n.p., n.d. Furnished by Mrs. T. C. McCorvey.

28. Letter of Julia S. Tutwiler to Nicholene Bishop, October 27, 1900. Tutwiler Collection, Alabama State Archives (Montgomery).

29. In the January, 1907, state certification examinations 51 of the 52 students of the Livingston Normal College taking them passed. Letter of Julia S. Tutwiler to Governor B. B. Comer, January 24, 1907. Comer MSS, Alabama State Archives. Julia Tutwiler, "Defects of the State Examination Law and Remedy To Be Applied," n.p., n.d. Tutwiler Collection, Alabama State Archives.

30. Records in possession of G. W. Brock. Letter of A. R. Meadows to Anne Gary Pannell, August 9, 1956.

31. Hyatt, *Development of Secondary Education in Alabama*, pp. 109-114. Jesse Monroe Richardson, *The Contributions of John William Abercrombie to Public Education* (Nashville: George Peabody College for Teachers, 1949), pp. 64-68. By 1910-11, however, all three

of the state normal schools had dropped their Association membership.

32. This organization was the outgrowth of a meeting of northern and southern ministers and educators first held in 1898 for the purpose of discussing how to improve southern education. Largely as a development from the sessions of this Conference, the Southern Education Board was established in 1901 to stimulate the campaign for free public schools. In April, 1907, Miss Tutwiler attended the sessions of the Conference for Education in the South held in Pinehurst, North Carolina. Letter of Julia S. Tutwiler to Governor B. B. Comer, April 8, 1907. Comer MSS, Alabama State Archives.

33. Julia Tutwiler, "Echoes from the Conference of Southern Educators" [incomplete memoranda], n.p., November 8 (no year). Typescript furnished by Mrs. T. C. McCorvey.

34. This was a complicated and lengthy process. Even as late as May, 1908, it was discovered that the Livingston town council had failed to convey to the state title to the new academic building and grounds. *Minutes of the Board of Trustees of the A. N. C.*, May 27, 1908. These records made available through the courtesy of Mrs. T. C. McCorvey.

35. Letter of W. H. Lawrence to Governor B. B. Comer, January 25, 1907. Comer MSS, Alabama State Archives.

36. *Minutes of the Board of Trustees of the A. N. C.*, April 16, 1907.

37. In order to facilitate the transfer of school land and property to the state, Julia Tutwiler advanced $2,500 of her own money to retire a bonded mortgage. She did this impulsively without securing any legal provision for repayment by the state. It is somewhat typical of her trusting nature that she apparently expected to be repaid by the state in payments approximating "rent." Statement of James L. Parker, April 15, 1907, appended to the *Minutes of the Board of Trustees of the A. N. C.*, April 16, 1907, but not referred to. Parker had been a trustee under the former regime. Signed statement of Thomas G. Makin, business manager, Feb. 13, 1908. Typescript furnished by Mrs. T. C. McCorvey. In the letter of T. M. Tartt to the Chairman of the Educational Committee, Montgomery, Ala., August 3, 1923, the statement is made that Julia Tutwiler never asked for the refund of this money and wouldn't have accepted it if the funds had been offered by the state. Typewritten copy furnished by Mrs. T. C. McCorvey. Julia Tutwiler also prepared a lengthy "Business Statement," n.d., setting forth her financial practices as president of the normal school. She was at pains to combat the idea that she was

a woman of wealth. Typewritten copy furnished by Mrs. T. C. McCorvey.

38. Letters of Julia S. Tutwiler to Governor B. B. Comer, May 30, June 6, July 1, 1907. Comer MSS, Alabama State Archives. Letter of Julia S. Tutwiler to Judge P. B. Jarman, July 11, 1908; letter to P. B. Jarman and W. S. Nichols, July 24, 1908. Tutwiler Collection, Alabama State Archives. Jarman and Nichols were trustees.

39. *Minutes of the Board of Trustees of the A. N. C.*, May 27, 1909; May 26, 1910.

40. *Minutes of the Board of Trustees of the A. N. C.*, May 6, 1907; May 27, 1908. Brock was a graduate of the State Normal College at Florence and of the University of Alabama. He had been a member of the first state teacher certification board and from 1902-07 had been superintendent of schools in Opelika, Alabama. *Announcement and Catalogue of the Livingston Normal College, 1907-1908*, p. 22.

41. G. W. Brock, *A Brief Sketch of the Livingston State Teachers College* (1936). Alabama State Archives. Interview of G. W. Brock by C. L. Pitts, cited in Pitts, "Tutwiler," p. 120.

42. Letter of Julia S. Tutwiler to Governor B. B. Comer, April 18, 1907. Comer MSS, Alabama State Archives.

43. *Minutes of the Board of Trustees of the A. N. C.*, May 26, 1910.

44. Unsigned and undated letter of Mrs. T. C. McCorvey to Nicholene Bishop. Copy furnished by Miss Bishop to Anne Gary Pannell.

45. Interview with G. W. Brock by C. L. Pitts, cited in Pitts, "Tutwiler," pp. 126-127. See Chapter 4 for an account of how early in 1910 Miss Tutwiler, aided by friends, endeavored unsuccessfully to secure a Carnegie teacher's pension. Letters in possession of P. A. Smith of Birmingham and Mrs. T. C. McCorvey.

46. *Our Southern Home* (Livingston), June 1, 1910. In view of the already strained relations it was particularly unfortunate that this portrait disappeared from the school within a year. Letter of Mrs. D. P. Culp of Livingston to Anne Gary Pannell. Pitts, "Tutwiler," p. 128.

4. ARDENT SPIRIT

1. Frank Willis Barnett in the *Birmingham News*, January 21, 1923.

2. Letter of President Ralph B. Draughon to Anne Gary Pannell, August 12, 1955. Until 1899 the name was the State Agricultural and

Mechanical College at Auburn. In 1959, the Legislature approved changing the name to Auburn University.

3. Much of the credit for securing the actual passage of the bill in the legislature should go to its sponsor, the Honorable Sol D. Block of Wilcox County. Later Block gave himself most of the credit for the establishment of the school and denied he knew anything about Miss Tutwiler or her work. His views appear in *Technala* [a publication of the school], 1921, p. 102, cited in Orr, *State Supported Colleges for Women,* pp. 131-132. The first name of this new school was the Alabama Girls' Industrial School. In 1911 this was changed to the Alabama Girls' Technical Institute. A further change to The Alabama Technical Institute and College for Women was made in 1919. This was shortened to Alabama College for Women in 1923.

4. In 1870 or 1871 the board of trustees of the University had considered the question whether or not the state was "equally bound to provide University education for its women as for its men." The decision at that time was against the admission of women to the University but in favor of the encouragement of their admission to normal schools and "theoretical and practical horticultural classes." Cited in James B. Sellers, *History of the University of Alabama, 1818-1902,* I, (University, Ala.: University of Alabama Press, 1953), pp. 474-475.

5. Julia S. Tutwiler, "A Paper on Co-Education and Character," privately printed, an address given to the Alabama Educational Association during its July 1-3 sessions in 1891.

6. Interview with Miss Nicholene Bishop, cited in Pitts, "Tutwiler," p. 164. Julia S. Tutwiler, "How the Girls of Alabama Pushed Open the Doors of the State University: Some Ancient History," n.p., n.d. Tutwiler Collection (University). Much of our information comes from this undated MS article.

7. "Alabama Has High Ranking in Education for Women" [article], *Centennial Magazine, Crimson-White,* 1931.

8. *Our Southern Home* (Livingston), September 29, October 6, November 10, 1898.

9. *Eutaw News,* November 25, 1880. *Montgomery Advertiser,* December 9, 1880.

10. Hardynia K. Norville in the *Alabama White Ribbon* (W.C.T.U.), March, 1940.

11. Interview with Mrs. Z. W. Sledge, cited in Pitts, "Tutwiler," pp. 195-196. *Livingston Journal,* December 20, 1885. Miss Tutwiler's own article on "Our Brothers in Stripes" in the NEA *Journal of*

Proceedings and Addresses for 1890 contains a great deal of information about her prison work.

12. Pitts, "Tutwiler," pp. 194, 196-198. In James B. Sellers, *The Prohibition Movement in Alabama, 1702 to 1943* (Chapel Hill: University of North Carolina Press, 1943), p. 53, the statement is made that an official state-wide W.C.T.U. organization was not formed until January, 1894.

13. Jane Zimmerman, "The Penal Reform Movement in the South during the Progressive Era, 1890-1917," *Journal of Southern History,* XVII (November, 1951), p. 482.

14. Henry Lee Hargrove, *Julia S. Tutwiler of Alabama: 1841-1916,* n.p., n.d., privately printed.

15. Much of the information here presented on the early prison schools comes from an account by Julia Tutwiler entitled "Report on Prison and Jail Work Among Miners," a *Supplement to the Minutes of the W. C. T. U. for 1887.* Typescript in Tutwiler Collection (University).

16. NEA *Journal of Proceedings and Addresses: 1890,* p. 605.

17. *Alabama's Report at the International Historical Congress of Charities and Corrections at Chicago* (1893). Alabama State Archives.

18. Letters of Julia S. Tutwiler to Governor B. B. Comer, July 1, October 9, 1907; March 22, 1909. Comer MSS, Alabama State Archives.

19. Newspaper clipping, n.p., April 9, 1911. Interview with Miss Tutwiler by Rosalie Armstead Higgins, from the scrapbook of Elizabeth Haley Moore. *Montgomery Advertiser,* December 10, 1911.

20. Letter of Julia S. Tutwiler to Bishop John Heyl Vincent, December 18, 1908. Typescript furnished by Mrs. T. C. McCorvey.

21. From the *White Ribbon* (W.C.T.U.), n.d. Typewritten copy furnished by Mrs. T. C. McCorvey.

22. For her account of Julia Tutwiler's prohibition activity, Clara Pitts searched the files of two church papers and three secular papers for the years from 1878 through 1916 without finding any contemporary reference to Julia Tutwiler's work. The papers were: Tuscaloosa, Ala., *Times-Gazette,* Greensboro, Ala., *Alabama Beacon,* Livingston, Ala., *Our Southern Home,* the *Alabama Baptist,* and the *Alabama Christian Advocate.* In the *Montgomery Advertiser* of June 9, 1910, she found a statement to the effect that "Miss Tutwiler started a campaign which led to the banishment of the saloons from Sumter and two adjoining counties." Pitts, "Tutwiler," pp. 224-225.

Acts of the General Assembly of Alabama (1886-1887). Information furnished by Mrs. Ruby P. Tartt, August 12, 1955. Mrs. Tartt also found that the act was printed in full, with the fines, in the December 23, 1886, issue of the *Livingston Journal*. She believes two reasons account for the absence of newspaper reference to these temperance efforts of Miss Tutwiler. One was her own modesty and dislike of publicity. The other was the fact that there was only one local paper and the editor was relatively free to print what he was interested in. In a letter of December 5, 1930, to Mrs. Marie Bankhead Owen, Mrs. Elise C. Ward states that as a student of Miss Tutwiler's during these years she worked with her in this effort to close the saloons. See also the article by Helen Christine Bennett, "Julia Tutwiler," *Pictorial Review*, April, 1913.

23. Clipping, n.p., April 9, 1911, from the scrapbook of Elizabeth Haley Moore. Julia Tutwiler, "The Star-Spangled Banner of Peace," n.d. Typewritten copy furnished by Mrs. T. C. McCorvey.

24. Letter of Julia S. Tutwiler to Bishop Vincent, December 18, 1908. Tutwiler Collection (University).

5. JOURNEY'S END

1. Extracts from McCorvey family letters, October and November, 1910, in the possession of Mrs. T. C. McCorvey. Letter of Julia S. Tutwiler to Dr. Thomas Owen, April 14, 1911. Alabama State Archives.

2. *Mobile Register*, August 22, 1915. Interview with Miss Agnes Tutwiler by Anne Gary Pannell.

3. Dorothea Mayo et al. to Julia S. Tutwiler, March 18, 1916. Tutwiler Collection (University).

4. Letter of Mrs. Anna Hunter Little to Anne Gary Pannell, August 8, 1955.

5. Two unidentified newspaper clippings. Interview with Miss Julia Tutwiler (a niece) by Anne Gary Pannell. Tutwiler Collection (University).

6. Clipping from Birmingham paper, March 26, 1916. Clipping from Livingston paper, n.d.

7. Clipping from a Tuscaloosa paper, c. March 26, 1916.

8. "A Memorial, Not of Brass to Miss Tutwiler" [newspaper clipping], n.p. (probably Birmingham), n.d.

9. "Annotated Will of Julia S. Tutwiler," prepared August, 1916. Typewritten copy furnished by Mrs. T. C. McCorvey. In establishing this loan fund, Miss Tutwiler expressed the hope that the money might be used to operate a summer session to take advantage of part-

time employment opportunities "when the girls who need money for education can earn it by canning fruits and vegetables." In A. B. Moore, *History of Alabama* (Tuscaloosa: Alabama Book Store, 1951), pp. 559-560, it is stated she "bequeathed her property to the creation of a loan fund for Alabama girls at the George Peabody College, which came to be known as the Julia Tutwiler Loan Fund." See also the article by Frank Willis Barnett, *Birmingham News*, June 6, 1926.

10. This portrait by Edna Smith had been done from life in the months just before Miss Tutwiler's death. Clipping, n.p., c. April, 1917.

11. The place in the Hall of Fame went to General Joe Wheeler. Although the proposal to change the name of the college was popular with many women's groups, it did arouse some opposition. The Livingston town council in March, 1923, pronounced the proposals "ill advised." Copy furnished by Mrs. T. C. McCorvey.

12. Letter of Annie Grace Mellen to Anne Gary Pannell, August 7, 1939. Article by Frank Willis Barnett, *Birmingham News*, June 6, 1926.

Clipping from a Birmingham paper, September 1, 1929. *Birmingham News* clipping, c. September 15, 1929. Typewritten copy furnished by Mrs. T. C. McCorvey. Apparently, the school administration delayed too long in making the improvements and when one of the local banks failed in the spring of 1930, this Tutwiler memorial fund was lost. Letter of Mrs. Elise C. Ward to Mrs. Marie Bankhead Owen, December 5, 1930.

13. Thomas M. Owen, Jr., "Julia Strudwick Tutwiler," typewritten copy of a radio address delivered on June 21, 1933.

14. "Julia Tutwiler Portrait Unveiled at the University," *Alabama School Journal*, XXXXIX (September, 1931), p. 6. Article by Mrs. W. L. Murdoch, *Birmingham News*, May 11, 1931.

15. *Our Southern Home* (Livingston), June 3, 1937.

16. The Alabama legislature in September, 1951, created the Alabama Hall of Fame for the purpose of recognizing "the inspiration to be found in the lives and deeds of a people's forbears." Election is by vote of a board, set up under the act.

Bibliographical Notes

by ANNE GARY PANNELL

THE MAJOR REPOSITORY of materials about Julia Tutwiler is the University of Alabama Library, referred to in the footnotes as the Tutwiler Collection (University). It was enriched in 1952 by a collection of printed and un-printed source material collected by the foresight of Dean Eoline Wallace Moore of Birmingham-Southern College, author of "Julia Tutwiler, Teacher."

The University of Alabama collection contains most of the few preserved letters written by Miss Tutwiler as well as a number of her poems, and articles on various subjects, both printed and in her own handwriting. The hand-written material is hard to read because of Miss Tutwiler's penmanship. Some of the materials have been damaged, which has contributed to the difficulty of deciphering them. In most cases I had photostatic copies made for reference.

Another important depository of Tutwiler material is the Alabama State Archives at Montgomery where are deposited a few letters and manuscripts of Henry and Julia Tutwiler, several miscellaneous folders of typed and printed copies of poems and articles by Julia and Henry Tutwiler and a large and miscellaneous collection of newspaper clippings about them, scrapbooks about Julia Tutwiler and articles written about her and her father. The Archives also contain a collection of Livingston Normal College catalogues for the later years of Miss Tutwiler's presidency there. The Comer Papers in the Manuscript Room of the Archives contain some correspondence between Governor Comer and Miss Tutwiler. In the case of duplication of material, material in the Archives usually has been cited only when it supplemented the material in the University of Alabama Tutwiler MSS.

Some copies of family letters and various versions of Julia Tutwiler's poems and articles were examined and copied while in the possession of Mrs. T. C. McCorvey of Tuscaloosa, a sister of Julia Tutwiler. It has not always been possible to determine where the originals of these typed copies are at the present time. Neither has it been possible to date this entire group of material. Since Mrs. McCorvey's death, her grandson, Dean G. Burke Johnston, Virginia Polytechnic Institute, Blacksburg, Virginia, has permitted examination and use of the Henry Tutwiler manuscripts, memorabilia, and printed articles and the McCorvey family scrapbooks containing Colonel McCorvey's writings, newspaper articles and miscellaneous clippings. These had been willed to him by Mrs. McCorvey.

Letters concerning Henry Tutwiler as well as materials and sources of his student days in Charlottesville have been examined in the Alderman Library, University of Virginia. I am indebted to Mr. Jack Dalton, the then Librarian, and the staff of this Library for great kindness and frequent and repeated loans of secondary material.

The files of two Livingston newspapers, *Our Southern Home* and the *Livingston Journal,* as well as many other sources in Livingston, were assiduously searched by Mrs. Ruby Pickens Tartt for material bearing on the years from 1881 to 1916. For over ten years I have been deeply indebted to Mrs. Tartt for her continued interest and many helpful suggestions.

Many of Miss Tutwiler's relatives, students and friends have generously sent material, given interviews and answered queries. A list of those to whom I am indebted for this help follows: Mr. and Mrs. George Johnston, Mrs. George K. Little (nee Anna Trott Hunter), Dr. R. Irving Little, Mrs. Richard Little, Mrs. W. K. E. James, Mrs. May S. Strickland, Mrs. J. M. Atkinson, Professor Wade Coleman, of Tuscaloosa; Paoli Smith, Esq., of Birmingham; Judge Walter B. Jones, Dr. A. R. Meadows, the late Mrs. Marie Bankhead Owen, Frank Grove, Esq., of Montgomery; the Honorable Gessner P. McCorvey of Mobile; the late Miss Nicholene Bishop of Akron; the late Dr. Hallie Farmer, Dr. Milton Orr, the late Mrs. Elizabeth Haley Moore, the late Dr. Mary E. McWilliams, Dr. and Mrs. T. H. Napier, of Montevallo; Miss Agnes Tutwiler, Mrs. R. P. Tartt, the late Dr. George W. Brock, of Livingston; President Ralph Draughon, Dr. Jesse M. Richardson, of Auburn University; Dean G. Burke Johnston, Virginia Polytechnic Institute, Blacksburg, Virginia; Dr. W. G. Bean, Washington and Lee University, and Cabell Tutwiler, Esq., of Lexington, Virginia. President and Mrs. D. P. Culp of Livingston State Teachers College have recently furnished valuable advice and pictorial help.

I am also greatly indebted for information and many courtesies to the authorities and librarians of the following institutions: the University of Alabama, Tuscaloosa; the University of Virginia, Charlottesville; the Alabama State

Archives, Montgomery; the Library of Congress, Washington, D. C.; Alabama College, Montevallo; Birmingham-Southern College, Birmingham; Livingston State Teachers College, Livingston; Vassar College, Poughkeepsie, New York; the College of William and Mary, Williamsburg, Virginia; the University of Michigan, Ann Arbor; and the generous, long-suffering, understanding and helpful staff of the Library of Sweet Briar College, Sweet Briar, Virginia. Furthermore, Dr. James Sellers, a generous colleague in the history department of the University of Alabama, furnished me in the years when he was writing Volume I of the *History of the University of Alabama* with copies of material he had found bearing on Henry and Julia Tutwiler and the establishment of co-education at the University. Dr. Sellers has also answered many queries about possible location of general material.

There has been no extensive printed treatment of Julia Tutwiler, her life and contributions to Alabama. An unpublished dissertation by Clara L. Pitts, prepared for the degree of Ed. D. at George Washington University, 1942, is the major biographical study that has been made up to this time. For a detailed statement of the available sources see Appendix I.

At the Library of Congress in Washington, D. C., I searched the obtainable issues of various periodicals and newspapers for which Miss Tutwiler was reported to have been a correspondent or contributor in the years from 1873 to 1910. The results were slight but I located three children's stories and articles published in *St. Nicholas Magazine* (1875-76); three articles in the *Proceedings of the NEA* (1890-93); two articles in *Appleton's Journal* (1876); one article in *The Churchman* (1879); and one article in the *Journal of Education* (1882).

The newspapers located in the Tuscaloosa Court House,

especially the *Tuscaloosa Gazette* of 1916, were examined. Through the continued interest of Mrs. W. K. E. James a later search has been made of this material to locate supplementary items.

All photostats, notes, manuscripts, printed material and correspondence about Julia Tutwiler in the author's possession are deposited in the University of Alabama Tutwiler Collection for reference. (A completely annotated typescript of this book, giving full references for quotations, is placed in this Collection. Footnotes in the printed version were reduced to a minimum.)

I am indebted to the following persons for their continued interest and advice: the late Mrs. T. C. McCorvey, the late Dean Agnes Ellen Harris, Dr. and Mrs. R. E. Tidwell, Dean A. B. Moore, Dr. Charles Summersell, Mrs. W. K. E. James, Mrs. Walter Bennett, Mr. and Mrs. Hudson Strode, of Tuscaloosa; my brother-in-law and sister-in-law, Mr. and Mrs. H. G. Pannell of Montgomery; my long-time and valued research assistant, Mrs. C. Ray Bryan of Bedford, Massachusetts; Dr. and Mrs. Ben Reid of South Hadley, Massachusetts; Dr. Helen Dodson Prince of Lake Angelus, Michigan; Dr. Dorothy Stimson of Stonington, Connecticut; Dr. Allen Going of Houston, Texas; Dr. and Mrs. Burke Johnston of Blacksburg, Virginia; and Miss Martha von Briesen of Sweet Briar, Virginia, all of whom have read and commented helpfully upon various versions of this book throughout ten years.

MANUSCRIPTS

THERE ARE 24 folders pertaining to Julia Tutwiler and her father Henry Tutwiler in the Library of the University of Alabama. The material includes press-cuttings, correspondence, poems, business statements, speeches, abstracts, reports, songs, sketches, typewritten copies of speeches about Tutwilers and photostatic negatives and photographs.

Folder 1. Gift of E. W. Moore, 1952. Julia Tutwiler, "Let Me Go: The War Drums Soundeth," 1862, 1 p. typescript. "A song written by Julia S. Tutwiler and placed on her father's plate at the breakfast table in 1862, imploring her father to let her go to the army as a trained nurse."

Folder 2. Gift of E. W. Moore, 1952. Julia Strudwick Tutwiler, "Our Father and Our Friend," music by Edward Wiebe. On front sheet: April 29, 1886, "To Matthew Vassar Esquire, the founder of their Alma Mater. Tribute of love and esteem, the members of Vassar Female College."

Folder 3. n.d. Letter of Julia Strudwick Tutwiler to "Anna" on the death of Anna's newborn daughter. Included is the poem, "The Little Ones in His Heavenly Home."

Folder 3. Gift of E. W. Moore, 1952. Manuscript letters of Julia Tutwiler to her sister Netta, October 4, 1873, from Kaiserswerth am Rhein, Germany.

Folder 4. Gift of E. W. Moore, 1952. Manuscript letters of Julia Tutwiler to Netta, December 3, 1874, from Steglitz, Germany.

Folder 5. Gift of E. W. Moore, 1952. Manuscript letters and notes of Julia Tutwiler to Netta, February 17, 1875, from Steglitz, concerning plans for Netta to bring a party of girls to Germany.

Folder 6. Gift of E. W. Moore, 1952. Manuscript letters of Julia Tutwiler to Netta, March 27, 1875, from Steglitz, describing Good Friday in Berlin and discussing possibility of Netta's coming to Steglitz.

Folder 7. Gift of E. W. Moore, 1952. Manuscript letters of Julia Tutwiler to Netta, February and April, 1875, from Steglitz, concerning plans for Netta to bring a party of girls to Germany.

Folder 8. Gift of Mrs. Clara Horton Curry, n.d. Julia S. Tutwiler, "The Marriage of Atlantic and Pacific" [poem], January 15, 1902, 1 p. MS. Poem appeared in the *Selma Times* in February, 1902, and was reprinted in the *Union-Banner* (Clanton) on December 30, 1934. (Correspondence concerning the gift of this manuscript by Mrs. Curry, Clanton, is in the folder.)

Folder 9. Gift of E. W. Moore, 1952. Julia Tutwiler, "A Business Statement" [report to the Board of Trustees of Alabama Normal College], 1908, 5 pp. typescript.

Folder 10. Gift of E. W. Moore, 1952. Letter of Julia Tutwiler to Judge P. B. Jarman, trustee of Alabama Normal College, July 11,

1908, Livingston.

Folder 11. Gift of E. W. Moore, 1952. Julia Tutwiler, "Report to the Board of Trustees of Alabama Normal College," 7 pp. typewritten copy (p. 1 missing). Report appeared in two parts in *Our Southern Home* (Livingston), July 1 and July 8, 1908.

Folder 12. Gift of E. W. Moore, 1952. Letter of Julia Tutwiler to Mr. Hart, July 21, 1908, describing need for a dormitory for white girls of the Black Belt. Suggests asking Russell Sage Foundation for aid. J. S. T. recounts her long struggles, her feeling of sadness and failure in what she had hoped to do.

Folder 13. Gift of E. W. Moore, 1952. Letters of Julia Tutwiler to Messrs. Jarman and Nichols, trustees of Alabama Normal College, July 24, 1908.

Folder 14. Gift of E. W. Moore, 1952. Letter of Julia Tutwiler to Mr. T. M. Tartt, May 26, 1910.

Folder 15. Gift of E. W. Moore, 1952. Iris H. Weed, "Julia S. Tutwiler" [article], *American Magazine,* September, 1910, 3 pp. typewritten copy.

Folder 16. Gift of E. W. Moore, 1952. "Miss Tutwiler elected honorary member of Birmingham writers club" [clipping], *Mobile Register,* August 22, 1915, typewritten copy.

Folder 17. Gift of E. W. Moore, 1952. (1) "Movement launched to honor teacher and poetress" [clipping with picture of Julia S. Tutwiler], *Birmingham News,* June 6, 1926; (2) "Tutwiler influence on Miss Geneva Mercer, sculptress, who did the Tutwiler Memorial plaque for the State Capitol at Montgomery, Alabama" [clipping], *Demopolis Times,* July 19, 1933.

Folder 18. Gift of E. W. Moore, 1952. Mrs. Kitty Meriwether, "Sketch of Julia Tutwiler by her sister," n.d., 4 pp. MS (pp. 1, 2 and 3 missing).

Folder 19. Gift of E. W. Moore, 1952. Julia Tutwiler, "Defects of the State Examination Law and the Remedy Proposed" [draft speech], n.d., 5 pp. typescript.

Folder 20. Gift of E. W. Moore, 1952. Julia Tutwiler, "Echoes from the Conference of Southern Educators" [speech notes or comments], n.d., 5 pp. Written on the back of stationery of Hotel Patten, Chattanooga, Tennessee, and like many present-day speeches sounds as though written on hotel stationery.

Folder 21. Gift of E. W. Moore, 1952. Julia Tutwiler, "A Little Journal of a Little Journey" [speech], Biloxi, Mississippi, n.d., 10 pp. MS.

Folder 22. Gift of E. W. Moore, 1952. Julia Tutwiler, "Commodore Maury, the Geographer of the Ocean," n.d., MS.

ARTICLES, REPORTS, THESES

Farmer, Hallie. "Henry Tutwiler," *Dictionary of American Biography,* XIX (1936), pp. 76-77.

Fleming, Walter L. "Home Life in Alabama During the Civil War," *Southern History Association Publications,* VIII (March, 1904), 81-103.

McCorvey, Thomas Chalmers. "Henry Tutwiler and the Influence of the University of Virginia on Education in Alabama," *Transactions of the Alabama Historical Society,* V (1904), 83-106.

McKelvey, Blake. "Penal Slavery and Southern Reconstruction," *Journal of Negro History,* XX (April, 1935), 153-179.

National Educational Association. *Journal of Proceedings and Addresses: 1884.* Boston: National Educational Association, 1885.

———. *Journal of Proceedings and Addresses: 1886.* Salem: National Educational Association, 1887.

———. *Journal of Proceedings and Addresses: 1890.* Topeka: National Educational Association, 1890.

———. *Journal of Proceedings and Addresses: 1891.* New York: National Educational Association, 1891.

———. *Journal of Proceedings and Addresses: 1892.* New York: National Educational Association, 1893.

Pitts, Clara L. "Julia Strudwick Tutwiler." Unpublished Ed.D. dissertation, George Washington University, 1942.

Proceedings of the International Congress of Education of the World's Columbian Exposition: Chicago, July 25-28, 1893. New York: National Educational Association, 1895.

Tutwiler, Julia. "The Charities of Paris: What One Woman Can Do," *The Churchman,* XXXIX (1879), 240-241.

———. "Our Brothers in Stripes," *National Educational Association Journal of Proceedings and Addresses, 1890.* Topeka: National Educational Association, 1890.

———. "The Technical Education of Women," *National Journal of Education,* III (November, 1882), 201-207.

———. "A Year in a German Model School," *National Educational Association Journal of Proceedings and Addresses, 1891.* New York: National Educational Association, 1891. (Paper read at the annual meeting of the NEA in Toronto, Canada, on July 16, 1891.)

Zimmerman, Jane. "The Penal Reform Movement in the South during the Progressive Era, 1890-1917," *Journal of Southern History,* XVII (November, 1951), pp. 462-492.

GOVERNMENT PUBLICATIONS

Clark, Willis G. *History of Education in Alabama: 1702-1889.* ("Bureau of Education Contributions to American Educational History," No. 8.) Washington, D. C.: Government Printing Office, 1889.

Mayo, Rev. A[mory] D[wight]. *Southern Women in the Recent Educational Movement in the South.* ("Bureau of Education Circular of Information," No. 1, 1892, Whole Number 186.) Washington, D. C.: Government Printing Office, 1892.

U. S. Department of the Interior. *An Educational Study of Alabama.* Bulletin No. 41, 1919.

U. S. *Report of the Commissioner of Education for the Year 1877.* Washington, D. C.: Government Printing Office, 1879.

U. S. *Report of the Commissioner of Education for the Year 1880.* Washington, D. C.: Government Printing Office, 1882.

U. S. *Report of the Commissioner of Education for the Year 1883-1884.* Washington, D. C.: Government Printing Office, 1885.

BOOKS

Bacon, Corinne (comp.). *Prison Reform.* New York: H. W. Wilson Co., 1917.

Boone, Richard G. *Education in the United States: Its History from the Earliest Settlements.* New York: D. Appleton & Co., 1893.

Boyd, Minnie Clare. *Alabama in the Fifties: A Social Study.* ("Columbia University Studies in History, Economics and Public Law," No. 353.) New York: Columbia University Press, 1931.

Brackett, Anna C. (ed.). *Women and the Higher Education.* New York: Harper & Bros., 1893.

Brewer, W[illis]. *Alabama: Her History, Resources, War Record, and Public Men: from 1540 to 1872.* Montgomery: Barrett & Brown, 1872.

Brown, William Garrott. *A History of Alabama for Use in the*

Schools. New York and New Orleans: University Publishing Company, 1900.

Brubacher, John S., and Willis, Rudy. *Higher Education in Transition: An American History: 1636-1956.* New York: Harper & Bros., 1958.

Bruce, Philip Alexander. *History of the University of Virginia.* 5 vols. New York: Macmillan Co., 1920.

Butts, R. Freeman, and Cremin, Lawrence A. *A History of Education in American Culture.* New York: Henry Holt & Co., Inc., 1953.

Coulter, E. Merton. *The South During Reconstruction: 1865-1877.* (*A History of the South,* eds. Wendell Holmes Stephenson and E. Merton Coulter, Vol. VIII.) Baton Rouge: Louisiana State University Press, 1947.

Cubberley, Ellwood P. *The History of Education.* Boston: Houghton Mifflin Co., 1920.

Dabney, Charles William. *Universal Education in the South.* 2 vols. Chapel Hill: University of North Carolina Press, 1936.

Davis, Charles S. *The Cotton Kingdom in Alabama.* Montgomery: Alabama State Department of Archives and History, 1939.

Dexter, Edwin Grant. *A History of Education in the United States.* New York: Macmillan Co., 1904.

DuBose, John Witherspoon. *Alabama's Tragic Decade: Ten Years of Alabama: 1865-1874,* ed. James K. Greer. Birmingham: Webb Book Co., 1940.

Elsbree, Willard S. *The American Teacher: Evolution of a Profession in a Democracy.* New York: American Book Co., 1939.

Finch, Edith. *Carey Thomas of Bryn Mawr.* New York: Harper & Bros., 1947.

Finney, Ross L. *A Brief History of the American Public School: A Genetic Study of Principles, Practices, and Present Problems.* New York: Macmillan Co., 1924.

Foerster, Norman. *The American State University.* Chapel Hill: University of North Carolina Press, 1937.

Going, Allen Johnston. *Bourbon Democracy in Alabama: 1874-1890.* University, Ala.: University of Alabama Press, 1951.

Good, H. G. *A History of Western Education.* New York: Macmillan Co., 1947.

Hyatt, Oscar W. *The Development of Secondary Education in Alabama Prior to 1920.* Nashville: George Peabody College for Teachers, 1933.

Knight, Edgar W. (ed.). *A Documentary History of Education in the*

South Before 1860. Vol. III: *The Rise of the State University.* Chapel Hill: University of North Carolina Press, 1952.

────── (ed.). *A Documentary History of Education in the South Before 1860.* Vol. IV: *Private and Denominational Efforts.* Chapel Hill: University of North Carolina Press, 1953.

──────. *Public Education in the South.* Boston: Ginn & Co., 1922.

Lange, Helene. *Higher Education of Women in Europe.* Translated by L. M. Klemm. New York: D. Appleton & Co., 1890.

Lossing, Benson J. *Vassar College and Its Founder.* New York: C. A. Alvord, Printer, 1867.

Moore, Albert Burton. *History of Alabama.* Tuscaloosa: Alabama Book Store, 1951.

Moore, Ernest Carroll. *Fifty Years of American Education: A Sketch of the Progress of Education in the United States from 1867 to 1917.* Boston: Ginn & Co., 1917.

Moos, Malcolm C. *State Penal Administration in Alabama.* University, Ala.: Bureau of Public Administration, 1942.

Newcomer, Mabel. *A Century of Higher Education for American Women.* New York: Harper & Bros., 1959.

Noble, Stuart G. *A History of American Education.* New York: Farrar & Rinehart, 1938.

Norris, Mary Harriott. *The Golden Age of Vassar.* Poughkeepsie: Vassar College, 1915.

Orr, Milton Lee. *State Supported Colleges for Women.* Nashville: George Peabody College for Teachers, 1930.

Osterweis, Rollin G. *Romanticism and Nationalism in the Old South.* New Haven: Yale University Press, 1949.

Owen, Marie Bankhead. *Alabama: A Social and Economic History of the State.* Montgomery: Dixie Book Co., Inc., 1938.

Owsley, Frank Lawrence. *Plain Folk of the Old South.* Baton Rouge: Louisiana State University Press, 1949.

Paulsen, Friedrich. *German Education, Past and Present.* Translated by T. Lorenz. New York: Charles Scribner's Sons, 1908.

Rice, Jessie Pearl. *J. L. M. Curry: Southerner, Statesman and Educator.* New York: Columbia University Press, 1949.

Richardson, Jesse Monroe. *The Contributions of John William Abercrombie to Public Education.* Nashville: George Peabody College for Teachers, 1949.

Riley, Rev. B[enjamin] F[ranklin]. *Alabama As It Is: or, The Immigrant's and Capitalist's Guide Book to Alabama.* Montgomery: W. C. Holt, Published for the State, 1887.

Robinson, Louis N. *Penology in the United States.* Philadelphia: John C. Winston Co., 1922.

Rogers, Agnes. *Vassar Women: An Informal Study.* Poughkeepsie: Vassar College, 1940.

Ryan, W. C., Gwynn, J. M., and King, A. K. (eds.). *Secondary Education in the South.* Chapel Hill: University of North Carolina Press, 1946.

Schmidt, George P. *The Liberal Arts College: A Chapter in American Cultural History.* New Brunswick: Rutgers Univ. Press, 1957.

Seeley, Levi. *The Common-School System of Germany and Its Lessons to America.* New York: E. L. Kellogg & Co., 1896.

Sellers, James B. *History of the University of Alabama, 1818-1902,* Vol. I. University, Ala.: University of Alabama Press, 1953.

——. *The Prohibition Movement in Alabama, 1702 to 1943.* Chapel Hill: University of North Carolina Press, 1943.

Sewall, May Wright. (ed.). *The World's Congress of Representative Women. . . .* Chicago: Rand, McNally & Co., 1894.

Simkins, Francis Butler. *A History of the South.* New York: Alfred A. Knopf, Inc., 1956.

Somers, Robert. *The Southern States Since the War: 1870-1.* London and New York: Macmillan Co., 1871.

Walz, John A. *German Influence in American Education and Culture.* Philadelphia: Carl Schurz Memorial Foundation, Inc., 1936.

Vincent, John H. *The Chautauqua Movement.* Boston: Chautauqua Press, 1886.

Woodward, Comer Vann. *Origins of the New South: 1877-1913.* (*A History of the South,* eds. Wendell Holmes Stephenson and E. Merton Coulter, Vol. IX.) Baton Rouge: Louisiana State University Press, 1951.

Woody, Thomas. *A History of Women's Education in the United States.* 2 vols. Lancaster, Pa.: Science Press, 1929.

Index